Entrepreneurship from Theory to Fact - Obstacles and Challenges in the Case of Sonia Amer ™

Entrepreneurship from Theory to Fact - Obstacles and Challenges in the Case of Sonia Amer ™

SONIA AMER

PARTRIDGE
A Penguin Random House Company

To order additional copies of this book, contact
Toll Free 800 101 2657 (Singapore)
Toll Free 1 800 81 7340 (Malaysia)
orders.singapore@partridgepublishing.com

www.partridgepublishing.com/singapore

Contents

Statement of Originality

I n presenting this dissertation for assessment, I declare that it is a final copy including any last revisions. I also declare that it is entirely the result of my own work other than where sources are explicitly acknowledged and referenced within the body of the text, and endnotes. This dissertation has not been previously submitted for any degree at this or any other institution.

Signature: Sonia Amer
Date:18/12/2011

Abstract

The topic of this dissertation is the way Sonia Amer implemented an entrepreneurship, the problems the trademark faced and the solutions provided by its management. The objective of the research is to help entrepreneurs to avoid start-up obstacles through the development of a practical business plan. Simultaneously, Sonia as an entrepreneur will learn from the feedback received, how to improve her entrepreneurship characteristics. The question to be answered in this dissertation is: What are the limitations of the entrepreneur's role in implementation of an entrepreneurship while creating an organization? Gartner's themes of entrepreneurship framework (1990) has been adopted and used as a foundation for answering the research question. The Gartner's themes of entrepreneurship where the answers will navigate within are: the entrepreneur, the innovation, the organization creative, the creating value, is the organization profit or not profit, the growth, the uniqueness and the owner manager.

The one case study research method has been chosen due to the exploration and qualitative nature of the research provided which requires deep investigation and analysis. The study depended on quantitative and qualitative approaches in collecting the primary and the secondary data, for ensuring the credibility and authenticity of the information provided. The tool used for collecting the quantitative data was the questionnaire; the technique used for collecting the qualitative data was interviews. The questionnaire and the interviews were considered primary data due to their validity. The printed books, magazines, studying materials and the internet have been used as tools for collecting the secondary data.

The data analysis paralleled with the data collected from the business plan provided by Sonia Amer. The findings highlighted the nonconformities based on the business activities investigated and Gartner's themes of entrepreneurship. The main findings were the lack of proper and continual funding, an unclear marketing strategy, overlapping the meaning of the value added between the product and the entrepreneur behavior.

As a conclusion of the dissertation, creating organizations requires innovation and control. Thus, in order to have another opinion for comparison, the writer of the research recommended further research in the limitations of the entrepreneur in funding new ventures, marketing strategies, creating organizations and adding values.

Statement of Authenticity

All the information, figures and tables of this dissertation are owned and provided by the owner of Sonia Amer trademark, the author. The primary collected data as well as the questionnaires are available in Sonia Amer ™ correspondences. Some information has been mentioned earlier, in the assessments of the marketing and entrepreneurship courses.

Abbreviations

AWSA: Arab Women's Solidarity Association Belgium
IP: Intellectual Property
ISO: International Organization for Standardization
MAP: Modern Portfolio theory
ROI: Revenue of Investment
SWOT: Strengths, Weaknesses, Opportunities, and Threats
TM: Trade Mark
WIPO: World Intellectual Property Organization
KPI's: Key Performance Indicators
NCR: Non Conformity Report

List of Tables

List of Figures

CHAPTER 1

Introduction

Sonia Amer ™ is an example of an entrepreneur's new ventures, designs, manufactures and marketing of ladies leather handbags, registered in Beirut in March of 2009. Operations started in Kuwait with a capital of $120,000 invested, with an expansion plan to include more countries within the coming five years. While implementing the business plan, barriers started appearing: the worldwide economic crisis of 2008, very high competition, deep funding problems, high manufacturing prices, finishing problems, obvious brand resistance, dissatisfied customers, lack of awareness, wrong advertisement campaigns were implemented (Brown, 2006).

The reason why the writer of this dissertation is interested in this specific topic is that she wanted to provide the knowledge she gained from her own business experience to other entrepreneurs as well as to her colleagues in Robert Kennedy College who wish to be entrepreneurs. The writer wanted to share her experience with them in order to help them avoid the start up business problems she went through. At the same time, the writer wants to learn from the feedback she will receive from the professors' comments. The dissertation is based on a fresh entrepreneur experience, a student of Robert Kennedy College who's struggling to succeed in a vary changeable environment "Why should we use our valuable time creating a document that tries to look into the future while the world is changing around us?" Brown (2006, p.1). The importance of this dissertation is the exploration of the limited role of the entrepreneur in implementing the entrepreneurship due to many related elements not under the entrepreneur's control, such as the variable external pressure in the fast and changeable macroeconomic environment we are facing (Moss, 2007). The dissertation as well suggests ultimate solutions to the barriers entrepreneurs might face while creating their own business.

The research question which has been answered is "What are the limitations of the entrepreneur's role in implementation of an entrepreneurship while creating an organization?" The writer of the dissertation argued that the entrepreneur is the first and main element of the entrepreneurship implementation, but the entrepreneur is just one element of eight important elements of the entrepreneurship implementation. The answer came as a result of the investigation made into the entrepreneurship implementation Sonia Amer trademark case study. According to the findings, the internal barriers such as the lack of funding and marketing strategies, and the external barriers which are out of the entrepreneur's control were also instrumental factors to be considered. The writer chose her own business as a case study for three reasons. The first reason is the lack of research covering the small size business ventures. The existing research mainly covers large business category for more clarity and credibility (Zahra *et al.,* 1999). The second reason is enhancing the qualitative approach in conducting exploratory research by focusing on one case study rather than many cases, which may lead to vague results and incredible evidences (Yin, 1994). The third reason is a poor existing knowledge base (Yin, 1994).

The objective of this dissertation is to help entrepreneurs to avoid start-up obstacles through developing a well prepared business plan. "Entrepreneurship, From Theory to Fact" has been chosen as a title for this dissertation to highlight the difficulties of shifting entrepreneurship from theory to practice. In order to define the barriers of implementing entrepreneurship, while creating our own organizations, we needed to define our roles as entrepreneurs by answering the research question.

Gartner's themes of entrepreneurship framework (1990) have been adopted as a foundation for answering the research question. According to Gartner (1989) entrepreneurship is a multidimensional process and that entrepreneurial traits constitute just one component of that process. That's why Gartner (1989) called for studies that build on the previous literature and developed theories for the study of the entrepreneurship process. Gartner's theory (1990) insisted that the organizations also behave, that the entrepreneurship is not considered an entrepreneur's behavior only, but that it is a group of eight themes and the entrepreneur is one of them, in addition to the innovation, organization creation, creating value, profit or not profit, growth, uniqueness and the owner manager.

Within the themes adopted in this dissertation, the writer clarified the differences between being an entrepreneur and implementing entrepreneurship. The important issues the writer started with are, the definitions of entrepreneur and entrepreneurship, the characteristics of an entrepreneur, and the elements of entrepreneurship such as; the strategic business plan, who is to be involved in preparing the plan and within implementation of it, the managing process and team, the leadership style adopted, maintaining innovation, the process of change, etc. The investigation and data collection relied on the literature reviews the writer found about "How to write a great business plan" as determined by Sahlman (1997, pp.29-56). How to prepare a business plan, how to approve it, whom to involve, how to stick to it during the implementation, and when to change the plan without affecting the innovation, leadership style and strategic planning - in other words how we can write a practical and realistic business plan that we can implement as specified by Brown (2006).

As stated by Patton (2002) the credibility of the one case study research method chosen is based on the primary data collected from the questionnaire and the interviews, and the secondary data collected from books, magazines and studying materials. Plus, the qualitative research approaches implemented such as the competitors interviews according to Stake (1995), in addition to the customers' questionnaire which has been used as a quantitative approach. The writer of the dissertation investigated the evidence from the reports provided by the owner of Sonia Amer trademark, the case study selected, and as mentioned earlier in this research, the writer investigated the feedback from the customers' surveys, and the direct and indirect competitors' interviews, to fulfill the credibility and validity data collection required in the qualitative studying approach (Patton, 2002). Furthermore the writer confirmed the validity of the research by matching the evidence to the studying materials and other resources such as printed books and magazines, as well as on the Internet using similar research and websites considered as secondary data.

The areas that have been investigated were the characters of Sonia as an owner manager, her leadership style, in addition to the innovation, the business plan prepared in order to create the organization, the brand uniqueness, the added value, and the growth strategies. Likewise, the investigation went through the obstacles that affected the implementation of the strategic plan, appraised the changes the management made, and suggested ultimate solutions. Furthermore, the study highlighted the limitations of the entrepreneur's role in implementing entrepreneurship due to many internal obstacles and variable external pressures mentioned by Moss (2007) in the fast and variable macroeconomic environment we are facing. Further explanations have been mentioned in the research, for better understanding of the strategy implementation, improving leadership style, innovation, shareholders stakes, and ways of funding. The rest of the chapters cover the following content: literature review; theoretical framework; research methodology; data collection and analysis; findings; conclusions and implications; limitations and recommendations.

CHAPTER 2

Literature Review

Many previous and recent researchers tackled the overall entrepreneurship subject, some researchers determined the difference between entrepreneur and entrepreneurship (Gartner 1988; Robins and Timothy, 2008). Some researchers divided the entrepreneurship into themes, they determined the meaning of each and every theme (Miller, 1987; Gartner 1990). Other researchers referred the entrepreneurship to the financial risk taking (Bhide, 1999; McCracken, 2011). Furthermore, some researchers linked the entrepreneurship to the well preparation and implementation of business plans (Brown, 2006). While, some recent researchers mentioned the importance of the Intellectual Property role in entrepreneurship, and the challenges facing the entrepreneurship (Amit *et al.*, 2007). Let us navigate within the literature reviews found, starting with the history of the entrepreneurship in order to have a better understanding about the subject:

2.1) History of Entrepreneurship: Some researchers such as Welfens (2002) explained the history of entrepreneurship. According to Welfens (2002) as per the new economy and economic growth in Europe and the US study, entrepreneurship history started in the 17th century as a result of the industrial revolution while more entrepreneurs appeared due to the internet innovation of the 20th century which made the electronic communication and supply much easier. Another research by Audretsch (2007) explained how the entrepreneurship became the proactive response to globalization. Audretsch (2007) clarified that the previous generations were loyal, they preferred to work with a sole employer for life due to the public policy and the social institutions which enforced security and produced labor force role in manufacturing plants. According to Audretsch (2007) it is not the case anymore due to globalization and new technologies which have encouraged knowledge more properties. Likewise, technology has encouraged knowledge-based entrepreneurship that is how the small business category has been considered the source of growth, innovation, jobs and competitiveness (Audretsch, 2007).

2.2) Entrepreneur and Entrepreneurship: The difference between the definition of these two words, entrepreneur and entrepreneurship, was tackled by few researchers. It was mentioned by Robins and Timothy (2008) when they stated that the entrepreneurs are the individuals with unique personality characteristics and abilities, in other words, entrepreneurs should be charismatic, able to influence others, they are usually stubborn, decisive, good negotiators and communicators and mainly, good listeners. While, Gartner (1988) mentioned two approaches to the entrepreneurship the trait approach and the behavioral approach. The trait approach depended on the entrepreneur characteristics, while the behavioral approach refers to the set of activities involved in creation organization. Gartner (1988) determined the entrepreneur as a set of activities involved in organization creation, while in the earlier trait approaches adopted by the previous researchers, an entrepreneur is a set of personality traits and characteristics. As per Gartner (1988) the behavioral approach has been considered a better approach to be adopted by the new created organizations, and he argued that the trait approaches have been unfruitful and that behavioral approaches will be more productive for future research in entrepreneurship (Gartner, 1988). From a different perspective, for McCracken (2011) what is most interesting about the entrepreneur is that an entrepreneur is someone who innovates although he will suffer. McCracken (2011) defined the real acts of innovation as something more than acts of combination. McCracken (2011) explained that those acts sometimes oblige the entrepreneur to leave the unrealistic idea about theory and practice and then become more logical. McCracken (2011) mentioned the difficulties entrepreneurs face, in his opinion it is not easy, and often, it is not fun, when the entrepreneur is forced to suffer, although it is not even profitable.

2.3) Themes of Entrepreneurship: In entrepreneurship theory and practices, Gartner (1988) clarified that to ask who is called an entrepreneur is the wrong approach, Gartner (1988) focused more on the importance of the other elements of entrepreneurship, which he called the themes, mainly, creating the organization, innovation, adding value and growth. Beside Gartner's themes of entrepreneurship, Miller (1987) highlighted the importance of the entrepreneurship themes such as innovation, leadership style, and strategic planning. Miller (1987) mentioned that after preparing, reviewing, and approving the plan, it should be transferred to a fact. Miller (1987) believed that the institutionalizing innovation means to develop systems that reinforce rather than inhibit strategic innovation in all the parts of the organization. Furthermore, Staten (1998) argued that the constant and leading organizational commitment to both gradual improvement and new creativity regarding profit creating activities, or at least facilitating a reduction of the cost of currently existing products.

2.4) Entrepreneurship and Financial Risk: Previous researches also covered the relation between new ventures and financial risk, especially in the case of profit business; without funding no ventures are built, as per Bhide (1999) business with over loaded liabilities are not able to survive. Bhide (1999) argued that the entrepreneur is a kind of person who is willing to take a financial risk. Bhide (1999, pp.1-28) also ensured that entrepreneurs must know their budget limit, they must reconcile what they want with what they are willing to risk. Bhide (1999) advised entrepreneurs to stick to their budgets in order to avoid any unexpected loss. Likewise, in a recent article about what-is-an-entrepreneur, an entrepreneur has been defined as an individual who accepts financial risks and undertakes new financial ventures. The article explained that the word derives from the French "entre" (to enter) and "prendre" (to take), and in generally the word applies to anyone starting a new project or trying a new opportunity (Wise Geek, September 4, 2011). Furthermore, in another article about writing a business plan it was also mentioned that the entrepreneur is the one who takes on the risk of starting a new business or creating a new product (The Money Alert, September 4, 2011).

2.5) Entrepreneurship and Business Plans: Gartner (1990) argued that Entrepreneurship is the creation of new organizations, starting new ventures, providing new ideas or preparing proposals/ business plans including the overall vision about the business suggested. The business plan has been defined as "a schedule of factors brought together to create a desired future" (Brown, 2006, p.7). Successful business was mentioned by Brown (2006) when he insisted that business plan should be practical, a business plan which could be implemented and works. Entrepreneurs should include in their business plan, the answers to the questions that could appear (Brown, 2006). A recent article about entrepreneurship ensured the involvement of proper planning and creativity. As per the article, the business plan should be structured in a clear way; it should include a summary, product or service, the project, management, technology, ownership, marketing strategy and market analysis, production or operation plan, and the funding sources (The Money Alert, September 4, 2011). As a part of the business plan preparation, Eddie and Maclaney (2009) focused on the budget and control, income statement, cash flow pro-forma and balance sheets. Kotler and Keller (2009) explained the marketing components such as the target segmentations, the direct customers, the intermediates, the competitors' analysis, the organization positioning, and the surrounding community circumstances. Kotler and Keller (2009) also defined the product, its specifications, its price, in addition to the places and promotions including its six elements - mission, means, message, moment, media, and measurement. Likewise, Robins and Timothy (2008) defined the persons to be involved according to their skills and experiences. Finally, the successful business plans included the Intellectual Property strategy (@WIPO/OMPI).

2.5.1) Entrepreneur and Delegating Tasks: What makes a successful entrepreneur is being a good negotiator and delegating responsibilities to the people involved in the venture (The Money Alert, September 4, 2011). Entrepreneurs are always negotiating, not only with customers, but also with other people who are keys to the business, like suppliers and lenders. Being a successful negotiator means you can always come up with a solution where everyone wins; no one walks away from the deal feeling like they were taken advantage of (The Money Alert, September 4, 2011). As a small business begins to grow, it becomes increasingly difficult for the entrepreneur to work alone. We need to hire people to help us do some of the business tasks. Otherwise, the quality of work may suffer because we are trying to do jobs we don't have the time or the skills to do. Even worse, the business could fail, if the entrepreneur is not diligent in checking the work done by others. Delegating the right work to the right people is a key factor. Still, it is not enough to delegate tasks and forget them. As entrepreneurs, we are ultimately responsible for the work done for our business. So, we have to make sure the jobs we have assigned are done on time, within cost, and at the quality we expect. We need to make sure our employees have the skills, money, and time they need to deliver what we have assigned (The Money Alert, September 4, 2011).

2.5.2) Entrepreneurship and Intellectual Property: Few previous researchers noticed the importance of the Intellectual Property role in the business progress and protection (@WIPO/OMPI). Recently, the innovation and small firms started taking more important role in the actual economic world, due to the technology revolution mentioned by Audretsch (2007). Recent researchers clarified the IP (Intellectual Property)'s strategy and its main role in supporting entrepreneurs' ventures, to define and protect the value of intangible assets satisfying the mandatory accounting and reporting "due care" obligations. The IP benefits are: realizing the ability to leverage/off assets, which are owned, but are not in use; better understanding of the market and market value of intellectual properties; reducing unauthorized use of IP by competitors and copiers; avoiding unauthorized use of other people's IP; providing the basis for a company culture based on innovation, brand presence and design. Intellectual Property strategy is a part of the overall business strategy - "strategy does not follow policy; rather strategy should follow the mission of an institution, while policy should be used to reinforce the strategy being purchased" (@WIPO/OMPI, pp.1-5)

2.6) Entrepreneurship and Future Challenges: Audretsch (2007) believed that the number of entrepreneurs increased, while their business is less secure because the governmental support goes to the big ventures instead of the small ones. Likewise, Welfens (2002) mentioned the future challenges facing entrepreneurs due to the globalization and monopolizing of the international companies. While, the effect of the innovation industry revolution on employment were mentioned by Zotan and Audretsch (1990). From Audretsch and Thurik (1999) point of view in the globalization and the telecommunication revolution, strategic initiating of the year long strategic plan are appreciated, it is required to initiate a year-long participatory strategic planning process to set goals and priorities for the business over the next five to ten years. One can use the strategic planning process to work toward alignment and attunement of internal resources by creating a schedule of development projects. Audretsch and Thurik (1999) advised entrepreneurs to continuously monitor the strategy implementation and evaluate results, making adjustments accordingly and keeping the process flexible. Audretsch, (2007) argued that although the competitive advantage has shifted to ideas, insights, and innovation, it is not enough just to have new ideas. It takes entrepreneurs to actualize them by adding them as values to the society (Audretsch, 2007). Also, the importance of the economic roles of entrepreneurship in the education and the society was mentioned by Bechard and Gregoire (2005).

As we can see the previous and recent research regarding the entrepreneurship theory and implementation proved that entrepreneurship is not a solo dance of an entrepreneur. Instead it is a harmony of a group of dancers such as the innovation, the product or service provided, the uniqueness, the created organization and the people involved, the growth and the added value (Gartner, 1990). It has been proved by the previous and recent research we went through in this chapter that entrepreneurship is mainly the organization creation, and the entrepreneur is the individual with the

CHAPTER 3

Theoretical Framework

According to the academic and exploratory nature of this dissertation, it requires the theory driven condition, the importance of the theoretical framework is the value of the analysis perceived. The discussion and the conclusions to be based on a theory is the main condition for gaining academic benefits from any research study. Exploration studies require logic, and depend on evidence to be investigated and deeply analyzed. Low and MacMillan (1988) in their study about the past research and future challenges of the entrepreneurship defined six design specifications for a research. According to Low and MacMillan (1988) the contributions and shortcomings of past entrepreneurship research can be viewed within the context of six research design specifications: purpose, theoretical perspective, focus, level of analysis, time frame and methodology. Low and MacMillan (1988) suggested a unifying definition of the field of entrepreneurship when they mentioned that the recent trend toward the theories defining the entrepreneurship driven research that is contextual and process oriented is encouraging. Low and MacMillan (1988) also argued that it is time for entrepreneurship researchers to pursue causality more aggressively. Accordingly, they discouraged the exploratory studies that are not theory driven, unless the topic is highly original.

The importance of the theoretical frameworks and concept applies in entrepreneurship research was mentioned again by Low and MacMillan (1988) when they suggested that research into entrepreneurial behavior should consider contextual issues and identify the processes that explain the implementation of it rather than merely describe the entrepreneurial theory. The focus of an entrepreneurial research on contextual and process issues was mentioned by Ucbasaran *et al.*(2000) when they suggested that future studies should focus on more precisely defined entities (example, a particular category of entrepreneurs), contexts and relationships. Ucbasaran *et al.* (2000) found that from a pragmatic perspective based on real experiences research, and précising a category of entrepreneurs in research, it may allow researchers to provide more specific advice and applications for entrepreneurs. However, the dissertation focused on Gartner's themes of entrepreneurship which have been chosen to be the dissertation frame work, in addition to the corporate culture which has been investigated as per the following:

3.1) Gartner's Themes of Entrepreneurship: different conceptualizations of the link between entrepreneurial activities and company performance were presented by Zahra *et al.* (1999) when they argued that large sample studies conducted in a wide range of corporate entrepreneurship and financial performance may yield different results. As per Zahra *et al.* (1999) those studies focused upon entrepreneurship as either an independent or a dependent variable. This concept also inflated the dissertation by linking the poor performance to the uncommitted team mention in the data collected. The writers insisted on the need for exploring different conceptualizations of firm-level entrepreneurship (Zahra *et al.*, 1999). While Gartner (1988) suggested that in entrepreneurship research the research questions should focus on the process of entrepreneurship instead of who the entrepreneur is. His implication is that entrepreneurship is a multidimensional process and that entrepreneurial traits constitute just one component of that process. Gartner (1989) called for studies that build on the previous literature and develop theories for the study of the entrepreneurship process.

The writer of this dissertation adapted Gartner's themes of entrepreneurship framework (1990) as a foundation for answering the research question: What are the limitations of the entrepreneur's role in implementation of an entrepreneurship while creating an organization? Because it is the most relevant framework to the issues the writer needed to highlight in this dissertation. Gartner (1990) determined the themes of entrepreneurship as per the following: The Entrepreneur is whom the entrepreneurship involves - the individuals with abilities, people who have unique and characteristic personalities. As per Gartner (1990) innovation happens when we do something new; it could be creating an idea, making a product, in a new or already established organization. Gartner (1990) explained that Organization Creation describes the behaviors involved in creating organizations, how to think, what to think about, whom to involve, where to get funding, the way we structure the organization and which is the best business plan to provide. Creating Values means to Gartner (1990) what is the added value we give to society; the entrepreneurship should create value. While, according to Gartner (1990) Profit and Non- Profit determines whether the organization is a charity or a profit business; however nowadays, profit business needs to have a cause, entrepreneurship does not involve profit making only anymore. Furthermore, Gartner (1990) considered Growth as a main requirement; we cannot run a successful business with no future growth, therefore growth has great importance as a characteristic of entrepreneurship. Also, Gartner (1990) involved Uniqueness in entrepreneurship implementation we need to avoid any overlap between the uniqueness of the product or the entrepreneur characters. And the finally, Gartner (1990) preferred the Owner – Manager, since entrepreneurship reinforces the involvement of individuals who are owners and managers of their own business.

There other reason why the writer of the dissertation chose Gartner's themes of entrepreneurship. While searching for books and articles about entrepreneurship, the writer noticed that in addition to Low & Macmillan, Gartner has a large amount of research related to the subject. Early in the 1988, he mentioned the difficulties of transferring entrepreneurship from theory to practice; he noticed the limited role of the entrepreneur as a sole in implementing entrepreneurship. Gartner (1988) excluded the trait behavior, what is called the one man show, because he believed in organizational behavior which has been reinforced lately by Robins and Timothy (2008).

3.2) Corporate Culture: Another side of the case study has been investigated, the company culture. How has it been built? How, and if not why? How has the portfolio been handled? What is the importance of prepared product portfolios and thinking-outside-the box as a business culture (Mani, 2006). Furthermore, how Sonia implemented the practical way to leadership. There are seven habits of highly effective managers: they need to increase their self-discipline; they need to show consistent kindness; they need to stretch goals; they need to welcome criticism; they must be a solution finder, not a problem- identifier; they need encourage boundless culture within the organization and grab opportunities (Carleen, 2007). The study investigated the way business problems have been solved, and judged it according to Gartner's themes. How to solve business problems when you "decide where you want to go with your business- and your life, uncover whether the business is in trouble and how much, overcome your cash crunch, quickly and forever, design a surefire blueprint for building big profits, end creditor problems for pennies on the dollar, without bankruptcy or borrowing, protect yourself and your personal assets from business liabilities" said by Goldstein (2005, pp.7- 8).

As a part of the company culture, the brand performance has been investigated, according to the themes of entrepreneurship adapted from Gartner. Revenue planning and its link with the brand's core competence and value commitments, policies and procedures, creating designs policy, implementing company knowledge base, maintain databases, employee empowerment, global competitiveness, standardization and network externalities, long-term growth, distribution and sales planning, market research and analysis, marketing plans and strategies, strategic relationships, and human resources all had to be considered in this dissertation. How the theory of entrepreneurship has been practiced, how the approved business plan has been implemented, who approved the business plan, the way the management has been handled, the style with which it was done. As per Johnson (2008) we should not leave our jobs, we do not need to rent fancy commercial premises, we should not be put off because we may be entering a downturn, we do not need to spend money on advertising, we do not need to rely on bank debt, we should not engage expensive advisers. Furthermore, Johnson (2008) advised us not to take on partners in a rush, we should not go ahead if our husband is against it, we should not be over-ambitious, we do not need to be lazy or impatient about research and homework.

Another important part of the company culture is the leadership style, the dissertation highlighted what leadership style has been adapted, as per McKee and Carlson (2005) task and people oriented or leading by objectives is the leadership style adapted, in order to increase relationships. McKee and Carlson (2005) encouraged the open door policy where they expected managers to be good listeners, transparent, supportive, authoritative, coaching, rewarding, motivating and encouraging, behaving and showing good attitude. At the same time, McKee and Carlson (2005) suggested that managers should influence power, should be good negotiators and have conflict solving skills in order to involve people by delegating jobs and responsibilities to them. McKee and Carlson (2005) encouraged managers to limit unnecessary control and to attend all training courses needed to match standard required, All these areas have been investigated and compared to the dissertation frame work.

The policies and procedures are the main component of the company culture, that is how, the study further investigated the level of clearness policies and procedures that have been determined, the internal business processes, the objectives and the measures used for continual improvements, the target and initiatives, the balanced scorecards, the financial sources, the customers, the competitors, the suppliers, the earning and growth (Atrill *et al.*, 2009). The study investigated the way Sonia had built the team; teams should be built by respecting each other while building trust and support, power and equalization, spatiality is only according to hard work and contribution, confrontation, and participation (Robins and Timothy, 2008). "Differences in organizational values within a top management team can impair how the group functions, with perceived differences having much larger repercussions than real ones" said by Robins and Timothy (2008, p.585). So, now that we have defined the study framework, let us move forward with the research to the credibility of the data collected, which has been insured as per the following research methodology.

CHAPTER 4

Research Methodology

After she went through many literature reviews about entrepreneurship, the writer found out that there is a lack of multidimensional researches which depend on both qualitative and quantities reports at the same time (Patton, 2002; Zaidah, 2007). Most research depended on either quantitative or qualitative approaches. According to Hopkins (2000) in quantitative research the aim is to determine the relationship between one thing (an independent variable) and another (a dependent or outcome variable) in a population. The quantitative approach has an objective nature and quantitative orientated, while qualitative approach is flexible subjective and qualitative orientated (Gillham, 2000; Zaidah, 2007). The case study research is the research strategy chosen in this dissertation. The writer choose her business as a case study, because, while searching for previous studies on the same subject, she found out that there is a lack of studies covering the small size business category where the writer's business belongs (Zotan and Audretsch, 1990). Mainly studies cover large size business for credibility and information availability (Zahra *et al.*, 1999). The few previous studies the writer found did not highlight the real importance of understanding the differences between being an entrepreneur and implementing entrepreneurship in the small firms under creation (Zotan and Audretsch, 1990). There was a lack of understanding of the difference between the theories of entrepreneurship and the difficulties of its implementation while creating a small firm (Zotan and Audretsch, 1990). Many areas needed to be clear for entrepreneurs, areas covering the implementation of entrepreneurship, the elements of the entrepreneurship, the relation between its elements, and the know how to use those elements to succeed in the best ways. The following subtitles explain why the writer chose the one case study method, the qualitative and quantitative approaches used, and the ways validity and credibility were handled.

4.1) The Research Method Implemented: For her poor knowledge in the business field and for better exploration and understanding business complex issues the writer chose the one case study research method (Gillham, 2000; Zaidah, 2007). Likewise, according to Yin (1993) the case study research design and methodology could be exploratory, descriptive, and explanatory. The explanatory research design method is our choice for this dissertation due to its investigation nature (Gillham, 2000). That is how, the study required the data collection to depend on the primary data collected from the case study selected documents, the questionnaire and the structured interviews (Gillham, 2000). The one case study required also to depend on the secondary data collected from the books, magazines, studying materials and some similar internet articles, Sonia Amer trademark and her competitors websites (Hox and Boeije, 2007). The primary data depends on the real experience of people, the experience usually is not documented or published, while the secondary data comes from the already documented although sometimes it is not published (Hox and Boeije, 2007). The dissertation is based on quantitative and qualitative approaches in collecting data for enriching the research with the multidimensional structure (Gartner, 1989). The validity and the reliability of the information came from the scientific form of collecting the data through conducting the questionnaire, the authenticity came from the methods chosen to analyze and interpret data (Gulnaz Ahmad hub page, December 18, 2011). The customers' questionnaire used for statistics and analysis, to get the feedback of the customers and analyze the reasons behind their answers. The questionnaires' analytical and statistical nature supported the study with the authenticity, credibility and academic validity (Best and khan, 1989; Blaxter, *et al.*1996). Likewise, the behavioral nature of the one case study required involvement of the top management and shareholders due to their responsibility and honesty. Those interviewees and shareholders provided information through structured interviews made by the researcher herself (Gillham, 2000). The structured interview has been also conducted with the competitors' sales and purchasing key persons. The investigation and exploration nature of the interviews supported the validity of the study, by getting the opinion of the people with the related experience, and understanding the market analysis (Delamont, 1992; Blaxter, *et al.*1996). Furthermore, the behavioral nature of the one case study required the qualitative content analysis as a method of examination of data material in order to integrate the qualitative content analysis into the data analysis (Gillham, 2000). The data analysis went hand in hand with the collected data (William and Veal, 2000).

4.2) The Quantitative Approach Implemented: As stated earlier in this chapter about the case study requirements "Quantitative research consists of those studies in which the data concerned can be analyzed in terms of numbers. Research can also be qualitative, that is, it can describe events, persons and so forth scientifically without the use of numerical data. Quantitative research is based more directly on its original plans and its results are more readily analyzed and interpreted. While, Qualitative research is more open and responsive to its subject" (Best and Khan, 1989, pp.89-90). Likewise, as per the ISO (9001- 2008) standards for performance measurement and continual improvement, the internal audit conducted required a customer survey which helped the writer to obtain and analyse customer feedback to explain and appraise each and every process has been audited. For gathering the primary data, in order to transfer the quantitative to qualitative information, the questionnaire has been designed in a very simple and clear way. It is based on directly relevant questions for ease of the customers' feedback analysis. It is one page length and it has six related questions with a small box beside each question to tick in and a suggestions box at the end of the questionnaire (Appendix no.1). The number of questionnaires received (forty three received) was considered satisfying for the management since the feedback included many categories of customers with different tastes and social levels. The structure of the questionnaire eased the finalizing of the indicators needed from the questionnaires as the indicators were specified and measurable, in a percentage measure, in order to simplify the data analysis. The sources of information used are the only available sources at the time and it is trusted by the trademark management.

4.3) The Qualitative Approach Implemented: Again, for the case study requirements "Qualitative research is concerned with collecting and analyzing information in as many forms, chiefly non-numeric, as possible. It tends to focus on exploring, in as much detail as possible, smaller numbers of instances or examples which are seen as being interesting or illuminating, and aims to achieve 'depth' rather than 'breadth'. On the other hand, Quantitative research is, concerned with the collection and analysis of data in numeric form. It tends to emphasize relatively large-scale and representative sets of data" Blaxter, *et al.* (1996, p. 61). And due to Sonia's limited knowledge in the sales and marketing, the interviews have been used to get the market study and competitors' knowledge in the local market. Likewise, the seven structured interviews have been handled with unified questions relevant to the subject (Appendix no.2). Direct questions about the market share, cost, margins and sales figures were included. The sales persons of the competitors were chosen to be interviewed for that sake and they have been interviewed directly or through the phone according to the interviewee's preference and schedule. The regular sales staff has been chosen as interviewees due to their practical experience, and their honesty; the high level managers will not give honest information in such a competitive market, seven interviews have been conducted by Sonia. Furthermore, one semi-structured interview has been conducted by interviewing the deputy general manager of Al Babtain Private Library.

4.4) The Validity and Credibility: Another concern has been taken into consideration, which is, to what extent the evidence provided is reliable for an academic judgment. To address this, the Balanced Scorecards concept has been taken into consideration. The audit conducted covered the brand from four perspectives: financial, internal business processes, learning and growth, and customers, in addition to the vision and strategy as the dynamo of the perspectives that links them together (MIT Sloan Review, January 17, 2009; The Balanced Scorecards Institute, October 31, 2011). Also, the writer developed metrics, collect data and analyze it relative to each of these perspectives (MIT Sloan Management Review, January 17, 2009; The Balanced Scorecards Institute, October 31, 2011). The thematic method has been used to facilitate understanding the aim of the dissertation and to reach its objective. Thematic method means merging the important themes and patterns in the data collected (Taylor and Bogdan, 1984). According to Aronson (1994) the first step in the thematic analysis is collecting the data in patterns. The next step to the thematic analysis mentioned by Aronson (1994) is to determine all collected data that relate to the already identified patterns. The writer used the thematic method, by collecting the data in patterns, and analyzing them in themes by identifying the data related to the already classified patterns (Aronson, 1994). Furthermore, the data analysis and findings based on the ISO (9001- 2008), ISO (the International Organization for Standardization) has been required by the brand's management, as a measurement tool for effectiveness and continual improvement (ISO, February 22, 2011). The KPI's (Key performance Indicators) has been implemented according to Kotler and Keller, (2009) and the SWOT analysis (Strength, Weakness, Opportunities and Threats) have been determined as per Brown (2006, p.14). Finally, the study included the limitations of the study such as the limited amount of information available and the required further investigation and future research to highlight the same findings from other perspectives.

4.4.1) Involving Shareholder: The data validity and credibility has been handled by involving the stakeholders. The data came from Sonia Amer brand's headquarter, such as the market analysis, printed materials, such as advertisement ads and leaflets, annual financial reports- the income statement, balance sheet and cash flow (Atrill and Maclaney 2009). The customers' survey and the questionnaires' design with its objective questions have been chosen and approved by the management before distributing it to the customers; the feedback and the results are available in the trademark documentation files. The documented interviews including the questions asked, the answers received, the date of the interviews, the name of the interviewees and their contact information are available in the trademark files.

4.4.2) The Academic Argument Source of Information: The academic books, journals, business magazines, notes, presses, and study materials have been used for ensuring the validity, to add value to the dissertation and to give it academic validity. According to the theories driven studies mentioned by Gillham (2000), the academic and theoretical driven research question based on Gartner's theoretical frame work mentioned earlier in this research. A sample list of some books the information refers to are in the following table which includes further the authors' names, books titles and dates.

I) Table 1: Books referred to in the argument.

Book Name	Author Name	Date
A Pragmatic View of Thematic Analysis.	Aronson, Jodi	(1994)
Developing a Business Plan that Works	Brown, Brian, B.	(2006)
Entrepreneurship Theory and Practice	Gartner, William, B.	(1990)
Entrepreneurship: Past Research and Future Challenge	Low, Murray B. and MacMillan, Ian C.	(1988)
Fieldwork in Educational Settings: Methods, Pitfalls and Perspectives	Delamont, S.	(1992)
Go it Alone with Style, Caution and Thrift	Johnson, Luke	(2008)
How to Write a Great Business Plan	Sahlman, William A	(1997)
How to Research	Blaxter, L, Hughes, C and Tight, M	(1996)
Innovation and Small Firms	Zotan, Acs j and Audretsch, David B.	(1990)
Institutional Innovation and the Future	Staten J. B.	(1998)
Introduction to qualitative research methods: The search for meanings	Taylor, S. J and Bogdan, R.	(1984)
Liquid people. Smart. Nice and Really Talented	Marty, Neomeier	(1996)
Pick The Brain	Luke, Ali	(2011)
Qualitative Research and Evaluation Methods	Patton, Michael, Queen	(2002)
Research in Education	Best, J and Khan, J.	(1989)
Solving Business problems	Goldstein, Arnold S.	(2005)
Successful Public Relations	Dunn, Jim	(2005)
The Entrepreneurial Society	Audretsch, David B.	(2007)
The Creative Edge	Miller, WC	(1987)
The Power to Change	Mckee, Rachel K. and Carlsoen, Bruce	(1999)
The Questions Every Entrepreneur Must Answer	Bhide, Amar	(1999)
Thinking Outside the Books in Company Culture	Madhu Mary	(2006)

These books have been used to gather the data in a way to cover the same subjects from more than one source. This strategy has been used to collect the maximum academic opinions provided on the topics approached by the study, mainly subjects related to the entrepreneurship theories and implementation in addition to many sample books in research studies, such as research methods and data collection and analysis.

II) Table 2: Magazines, Notes and Studying Materials referred to in the argument.

Magazines
Critique Magazine.
Journal of Management Studies
MIT Sloan Management Review (2008)
MIT presses (1990,1995)

Notes
The entrepreneurship, Harvard Business Review Cambridge university presses. Oxford University Presses, and the Emergency Response & Research Institute. Some information came from one paper called the Focus of Entrepreneurial Research: Contextual and Process Issues, about the Focus of Entrepreneurial Research Contextual and Process Issues, that paper had been presented in the Tenth Global Entrepreneurship Conference, March 2000, by the University of Nottingham Institute for Enterprise and Innovation. Mixed Sampling Definitions (OECD Glossary of Statistic Terms, 2002).

Studying Materials
The data collected from the studying materials of the MBA program, Robert Kennedy College such as, Marketing Management, Kotler, Philip and Keller, Kevin Lane (2009). Organizational Behavior, Robins Stephen, and Timothy, Judge (2008). Accounting and Introduction, Eddie, Atrill, and Maclaney, Peter (2009).

These magazines and notes about business implementation have been cited, in addition to the data collected from the studying materials of the MBA program, Robert Kennedy College for enhancing the argument and ensure validity, the table included the authors' names, subjects and dates. More detailed explanations are mentioned in the following data collection and analysis.

CHAPTER 5

Data Collection

As mentioned earlier in this dissertation, the research question "What are the limitations of Sonia's role while creating her organization?" was investigated within Gartner's themes of Entrepreneurship. The study investigated whether Sonia is characteristic of and if she can be considered an entrepreneur and an owner manager, how she created her organization, how she choose the people involved, if her business plan is considered a well prepared strategic business plan for creating a successful organization, what makes her brand unique and if her business plan included growth? The investigation also determined the obstacles which affected her entrepreneurship implementation and strategic plan, the modifications she made to her business plan, the reflection of her leadership style on the changes she made to the business plan, the ways she handled innovation, and to what extent she added value to the society since her business is a profit business. As per the research methods adopted in the dissertation, all these areas investigation clarified that the role of us as entrepreneurs is really very limited when it comes to the implementation of the entrepreneurship. That is how the dissertation objective has been insisted, to highlight the most important areas to be taken into consideration before getting into any new venture, and to avoid the new business start up obstacles. Besides having a very well prepared business plan. The writer collected the information, validated the information with the written collected documents, the business plan of Sonia Amer trademark has been considered the procedure, and the audit conducted in a subjective manner according to the procedures of the business plan, as per the following case study selection.

5.1) The Case Study Selected

As mentioned previously in this research, Sonia Amer ™ for genuine leather handbags is the case study selected with both quantitative and qualitative approaches, to dig into deep investigation and find out where things went wrong in order to share knowledge with other entrepreneurs and for Sonia Amer brand to improve its operations. According to Gartner's definitions about the entrepreneurship themes, Sonia's entrepreneurship characteristics gathered were: she is the founder of Sonia Amer ™, her ethnicity is Lebanese, she has been living in Kuwait for the past 23 years, she is an MBA student, and she is 40 years old. She has 12 years of experience in administration work and quality assurance. She is an employee with a full time job, with a law studies background. She is a painter, poet and Arabic stories author, a good listener, a decision maker and well connected to the Kuwaiti society. Her negative characteristics are: she is stubborn, tough and moody, finds it difficult to trust people, and is a high-risk taker. She is an owner manager involved in every single detail of the venture. She designs the ladies genuine leather handbags to be manufactured and sold under her own brand name, which is registered in her country, Lebanon. Uniqueness about her business is that it is the only Arabic brand with a purely Arabic product, from the designer to the leather used and the manufacturing. To create the organization, according to "How to Write a Great Business Plan" determined by Sahlman (1997. pp. 29-56), Sonia prepared a business plan. According to Brown (2006, p.7) the business plan is a "schedule of factors brought together to create a desired future". Brown (2006) named these factors: The Budget and Control, the Customers, the Competitors, the Shareholders and the Community. However, the writer of the study went through these elements as per the following information received from Sonia Amer™ management.

5.1.1) Budget & Controls: The essential investment was $ 120,000 in 2009; the fiscal year 2010 was not counted in the revenue expectations for growth reason and due to the startup expenses, and the worldwide economic crisis circumstances. According to Stancil (1997) the first question entrepreneurs should answer is how much money does their new venture need?. The business growth expected was 18 % for 2011, 20 % growth starting in 2012. The annual increase in direct and indirect costs plus fixed and variable costs have been taken into consideration (Eddie and Maclaney, 2009). The income statement, balance sheet statement, and cash flow statement were prepared in detail for the coming five years (Appendix no.3). Also, Sonia kept in mind that Kuwait is a tax-free country, while in Lebanon there is 10 % tax. She also maintained an accurate report covering the financing, sales, receivables and inventory reports. However, the actual income statement 2009- 2010 mentioned a loss of $4,087.

I) Figure 1: Actual Income Statement 2009-2010, resource Sonia Amer trademark's annual report 2009-2010.

	Actual Income Statement 2009-2010	
Sr. No.		**In American Dollar ($)**
1	Sales	31,745
2	Cost of Goods	17,708
	Revenue	**14,037**
	Operation Expenses	
3	Travel expense	3,300
4	Rent	5,824
5	Printing	3,000
6	Website Development	1,500
7	Advertisements	1,000
8	Registration	2,000
	Total Operation Cost	**16,624**
	Income Before Taxes	**-2,587**
10	Taxes	1,500
	Net Income	**-4,087**

5.1.2) Customers: The targeted customers in the business plan provided are the wealthy Kuwaiti women who earn more than $ 3000/- per month. The target segmentation of direct customers are: Kuwaiti women between 20 – 60 years old represents 60 % of Sonia's target, their life style of being up to date and trendy, well educated and uncommitted (Kotler and Keller, 2009). Teens aged between 15- 20 years old represents 30 % of her target, due to their lifetime value. Sonia wanted them to believe in the brand, to build a life-long loyalty (Kotler and Keller, 2009). The non-Kuwaiti women who earn more than $ 2,000 per month, represent 5 % of her target and they are about 5 % of the labor force in Kuwait (Kotler and Keller, 2009). The intermediates and indirect customers are: Men between 20- 60 years old which represents 5 % of her target; men who need the best hand bag for their partners to influence them (Kotler and Keller, 2009). The last customer target is companies as business complementary for creating a differentiation, generating publicity, cutting marketing cost and sharing customers (Kotler and Keller, 2009). Meanwhile, according to 2001 statistics, the category of 15-59 years old is the highest 53 % of the citizens, which is considered optimistic, while the female labor force is 31 % (Kuwait General Data, March 22, 2009).

5.1.3) Figure 2: Competitors and Market Share, resource, Sonia Amer trademark, business plan, 2009.

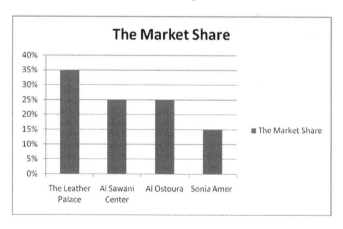

Figure analysis: the numbers presented in the chart are just an assumption according to the sales persons met by

Sonia in 2009 through the structured interviews. There is no official research, or written information officially published in that regard.

35% for the Leather Palace = 4,666 handbags

25% Al Ostoura = 3,333 handbags

25% Al Sawani Center = 3,333 handbags

15% Sonia Amer ™ = 2,000 handbags

The plan also mentioned the strategies of how to get there specified by Macmillan and Tampoe (2009). The strategic tactics according to Roc (1987) are the overall strategic questions each entrepreneur should answer. The ways of marketing mentioned in the plan are the direct retail to cover the targeted areas with reasonable and fixed prices, promotions, bundling, payment and credits facilities, word of mouth, on line shopping, a reverse policy, customer privacy and special edition orders, phone calls, home delivery, outdoor sales, marketing campaigns, after sales services, maintenance and cleaning used bags (Kotler and Keller, 2009). The marketing plan also included the brand scope of product line, which is ladies handbags and purses. In addition to the product specified features and benefits mentioned, and new designs were scheduled to be added to the collection each and every season.

I) The price range $150 to $ 600 per bag was suggested as a competitive cost (Brown, 2006), and developing implementable pricing strategies and programs (Kotler and Keller, 2009). Their prices are the most reasonable when compared to their competitors, the strategy behind that being that the price is to compete with the competitors by stealing 15 % of the market share (Eddie and Peter, 2009). The profit margin decided was 50 % as a beginning; the percentage margin is the percentage of the final selling price that is profit (Building Trade Organization, May 9, 2011). The 50 % margin is decided due to the opportunity of tax free law implemented in Kuwait, as well as the reasonable price of the raw material and work force for manufacturing in Egypt. Furthermore, Sonia adopted the fix price policy, for building trust and attracting customers; she adopted a flexible reversing and exchanging policy: inside Kuwait, within two to three days of receiving the product; outside Kuwait, within two to three weeks, but the shipment cost handled by the customer. Any money return cost is deducted from the amount paid.

II) The places and locations mentioned in her business plan as distribution channels beside the direct retail locations included, the distributors, intermediates, online, and over the phone (Kotler and Keller, 2009). The reason behind this distribution strategy is that Kuwait is a small country, which means the customer is able to reach any shopping mall in half an hour of driving. The promotions included the mission, the objectives of the promotions such as the awareness and recognition of the new brand, gaining the customer attraction to try the product and buy it again, stealing competitors' customers (Kotler and Keller, 2009).

III) The size of the promotions budget invested mentioned as 10% of their revenue in marketing $ 40,000/-, annual revenue is $ 400,000/-, taking the average of selling 2,000 bags per year (2 bags per day x 2 locations x 365 day = 1400 bags + 1 bag per day through Intermediary = 365 + Exhibitions 235 bags, average price $ 200/- per bag x 2000= $ 400,000/-), the ratio is $ 40,000/- divided by 40,000/- consumers = $ 1 per customer (Eddie and Peter, 2009).

IV) The message to be passed with each advertisement campaign was also mentioned in detail, one message at the right time, through the right media - simple, emotional and explanatory. The Logo is the African Elephant with his trunk up, considered a provider of luck, respectful, patient and strong enough to carry the heavy responsibilities for a long journey (Appendix no.4). "Bag your life" is the slogan to show the importance of the bag in the life of a woman, the media, according to the successful public relation (Dunn, 2005).

V) The measurement of the success and ROI (Revenue of Investment), revenue of each promotion is measured according to an awareness survey about brand recognition, trial and purchase (Invest Your Dictionary, October 30, 2011). Other activities include reviewing results quarterly revenue versus expenses, updating customer data bases, life style of Kuwaiti customers gained, rural or urban, nationalities of the gained customers, which nationality is increasing and why, which designs made the highest sales and why, which colors are preferable and why, which sizes are the most required and why (Kotler and Keller, 2009).

5.1.4) Shareholders and Internal Structure:

Sonia chose the Contribute and Commitment (The 9.9 style) in leadership style (Mckee and Carlsosn, 1999). Her team is virtual to some extent as one operation manager is located in Egypt for manufacturing needs, another operation manager is located in Lebanon for marketing and administration issues and sales ladies are distributed in Egypt, Lebanon and Kuwait. An Internet connection and phone calls are in use for facilitating operations; brainstorming meetings are conducted as per the need. This is the way the team has been built, as per the high performance organization, building enduring greatness through a paradoxical combination of personnel humility plus professional will (Harvard Business Review, July-August 2005). The members of the team are:

I) Consultant; Fadi Alam: Lebanese, 51 years old, 34 years of hotel management background, sales and marketing in addition to public relation, husband of Sonia; he is well connected to the Kuwaiti society, customers, sellers and authorities. He provided the main brand show room in Lebanon. His negative quality is that he is too conservative.

II) Operation Managers; Ahmad Mustafa, Egyptian, 52 years old, 35 years of sales and marketing back ground in the management and heavy equipment industry, Masters in air-conditions engineering, a family friend, financing the goods cost with 20 % interest to be paid within six months divided (10 % interest plus 10 % operation). He loves details; his negative quality is that he is a high-risk taker. His main job is to find the suitable factories, follow up with the factories for meeting manufacturing dates, and shipment details for fulfilling delivery deadlines.

III) Nader Amer, Lebanese, 30 years old, political studies back ground, he is the brother of Sonia Amer. He is not interested in his current job and having the ambition to have a better, public relation oriented career, excited about fashion. He is honest and trustworthy; he follows up the marketing progress, receiving goods from the airport, managing customizing issues and ensuring the accurate storage. He is very specific and loves details.

IV) Sales managers; Natalie Fadel is in charge of the Lebanon market, she is the wife of Nader Amer. She is 30 years old, a teacher with a law studies background. She has very good sales skills due to her family experience in the retail business; trustworthy, sharp and close to Sonia, she can also be ambitious and stubborn.

V) Majida Al Khalily is the team member responsible for the Egypt market. She is 49 years old, a house wife with a commercial studies background, sharp, honest, a close friend of Sonia and trusted by her; wife of Ahmad Moustafa.

VI) Distributors; In Kuwait, they are mainly sales ladies, 25 to 55 years old, hair dressers, tailors, shops owners, friends of Sonia, or people known in the market. The problem is that they are moody, lazy and the only way to get them to work is to pay a 20 % commission. Finding other distributors went on through an Internet search, mainly Linked In channels.

Many opportunities have been negotiated, such as Canada, through a Lebanese Canadian, Iran through an Iranian customer, Saudi Arabia through a Saudi distributor, and two deals have been finalized with two colleagues of Sonia in Robert Kennedy College, one in Singapore and the other in Tanzania (Appendix no.5).

To keep the team challenged, the business plan mentioned innovation; in order to market the brand well, they needed to settle and maintain the brand's positioning as stated by Marty (1996). Design drives innovation; innovation powers brand; brand builds loyalty; and loyalty sustains profits. If we want long-term profits, we need to start with design. Marty believes that design is a powerful business tool for building a successful brand from the inside and out (Marty, 1996). Sonia Amer™ is an Arabic leather handbag brand, but why does it matter? It matters because of the unique identity, discipline and focus, collaboration, innovation, validation, creation, strategic and conceptual, trusted and added value respects stakeholders, customer service oriented, business to customer concept, diversity environment, fair employment through advertisement and specific criteria (Marty, 1996). The business plan also mentioned the implementation of ISO (9001- 2008) as a measurement tool for effectiveness and continual improvement, continual training programs, motivating and implementing a rewarding system for attracting and keeping good employees.

5.1.5) Community: Sonia's strategy is to care about more than money; it's not selfish to put ourselves first. For human beings there are physical needs, emotional needs, mental needs, and spiritual needs (Luke, 2006). Sonia is an Arabic poet and author of stories; her dream is to publish her books and to establish her own literature salon to be a part of her gallery. She encourages literature, and supports women's rights by sponsoring AL Babtain Library's Prize - a well known private library that has a large audience, especially wealthy Kuwaiti women (Kotler and Keller, 2009). She shows her support by marketing her slogan (The Only Bag with a Poem). She sponsors the women's rights activities such as AWSA (Arab Women's Solidarity Association - Belgium), and the Kuwaitis' women forums. The reason for sponsoring is building the brand image and gaining trust, furthermore adding value. Keeping a good connection with the journalists, Kuwait TV and Radio where she's usually interviewed promotes her venture of designing and selling handbags, and promoting herself as a writer, painter and a designer for Darraas as a compliment to the original business of selling genuine leather hand bags. Darraas are traditional Kuwaiti women's clothes, similar to an Abaya. Environmentally, Sonia insisted that the leather used could be absorbed by the soil. Economically, although 2009 was a tough time to start a business, Sonia believed that it could be the best time due to the cheap raw material and workforce available in Arabic countries. Finally, Sonia has been chosen to be one of the founders of Thameen toastmaster club which includes the Listening club, the Reading and the Art of Life club. Those clubs are sponsored by the FA Gallery, a high class exhibiting show room for displaying paintings and fashion where Sonia is pushing hard to display her products. For social return and possible future earnings,

Kiva is one of Sonia's investment baskets, in addition to the Zakat investment 2.5%.

Now after the writer of this dissertation presented the data collected from Sonia Amer's business plan and annual reports, the writer needed to ensure the validity of the information received in order to give her dissertation validity and authentic value. The writer used the primary and secondary data collection methods, and depended on quantitative and qualitative approaches, the tools used are customers' questionnaires and competitors' interviews as per the following:

5.2) The Customer Survey has been used as a quantitative method for collecting and gathering data. At the same time, it has been used as a kind of measurement tool for the business performance and customers' feedback. The questions have been based on implementing the Balanced Scorecards objectives, measures, targets and initiatives in order to improve the ability of the brand to adapt to the changes in its surrounding environment, as per the following aspects: Vision and Strategy, finalizing and gluing all perspectives together; Financial, to succeed financially, and how the brand should appear to its shareholders; Customers, in order to achieve the management vision and how they should reply to their customers; Learning and Growth, to achieve the strategy and how to sustain the ability to change and improve; Internal business processes, to satisfy the shareholders and customers and what business process they must excel at (MIT Sloan Management Review, Summer 2008). The questionnaire is available in appendix no.1.

The results of the survey received are: 68 % found the product 'trendy', while 15 % found it 'classic' and 17 % found it 'old fashion'. 66 % found the price 'reasonable', 34 % found it 'expensive', while no one found it 'cheap'. 56 % found the quality 'very good', while 39 % found it just 'good', and 5 % found it 'bad'. 88 % answered the collection varieties could be used both 'casual and for evenings', 9 % saw it as 'casual' and 3% saw it for 'evening use only'. 95 % knew about the brand 'through a friend', while 5 % knew from 'other sources'. 66 % would 'recommend it to their friends', while 24 % responded 'maybe' and 10 % 'will not'. In addition, some suggestions were increasing the number of designs and decreasing the price (Appendix no.1). The received results led the management to review the brand's positioning and strategic plans, reviewing monthly the customer progress- if the number is increasing or decreasing, the quality of the customers gained, the life time value and loyalty. A customer survey is also helpful in analyzing the customers' needs and ensuring continual improvement in designs and service. Keep in mind that the questionnaire questions have been discussed with the management before being approved as a kind of credibility and validity and for ensuring that there are no missing areas to be covered. By sharing the knowledge of the management members and increasing the ownership feeling and the innovation atmosphere within the brand, the team suggested getting verbally the answers of the customers to be documented immediately and transparently.

5.3) The Competitors and Intermediates Interviews were used as a qualitative method of data collection as a credible and a valid way of gathering the data used in exploratory research for deep understanding and focus (Best and Khan, 1989). The criteria of the interviews decided were the structured interviews and the interviewees to be the competitors' sales persons, or managers (Gillham, 2000). Sonia chose the regular staff and medium management level due to their honesty because higher level managers will not provide the real information in such a competitive market. The writer of the study conducted seven structured interviews, and the validity and credibility have been handled through documenting the interviews, the questions and the answers received, the date when the interviews were conducted, the names of the interviewees and their contact information (Gillham, 2000). Sonia met the direct competitors' interviewees while doing the market search and analysis. Al Sawani, Leather Palace and Al Oustoura are the competitor companies. The interviews were conducted face to face for all the interviewees, except the customer service manager of Al Oustoura; the sales person met by Sonia was dedicated to Fransisco Biasia shop, although the brand is under Al Oustoura. All interviews were conducted on the same date, the 25th of March 2009. The names of the interviewees are confidential, as per their request. The questions were standardized as mentioned in Appendix no. 2. The questions have been discussed with the management members and approved before being asked to the interviewees (Gillham, 2000). Accordingly, the following feedbacks were received, the interviews questions mentioned in Appendix no.2:

5.3.1) Table 3: The Details of Interviews, resource, Sonia Amer trade mark's documentation, the interviews conducted, March, 2009.

Direct Competitors	Company Name	Establishment Date	Number of Locations	Interviewee
	The Leather Palace	1977	9 Locations	Sales Person
	Al Sawani Centre	1993	5 Locations	Sales Manager
	Al Ostoura Company	1985	8 Locations	Sales Person
				Service Manager
Indirect Competitors				
	Comfort Shoe Co.	Late Eighties	More than 5 Locations	Sales Manager
	Steps Co.	Late Eighties	More than 10 Locations	Purchasing Manger
Intermediates				
	Golden Galaxy Company	1 Location	1990	Sales Person
Complementary Business				
	Al Babtain Library	The Deputy General Manager		

I) - The Leather Palace Company specializes in handbags only, including Samba for bags and shoes and Plus IT for bags, shoes and accessories. It is a limited company established in 1977, with nine locations. Their strengths are the number of show rooms they own, they are well known, they have internationally branded handbags, such as; Cavali, Gean Frank Ferre, Lincester de la Roche, Juliana, Custome National, Pontatrace and Cromina which is 100 % real calf leather, goat, sheep and cobra skins. Prices range from $ 300 to $ 750. They represent about 40 % of the local market share for this category. Their level is below international designers and above Next, Zarra, Steps, Mexx, etc. They advertise through Al Watan, Al Qabas, Al Anbaa newspapers, and Samra monthly magazine (Kotler and Keller, 2009).

II) - Al Sawani Center including Rocco Barocco and Furla Boutique, a limited company established in 1993, specializing in leather handbags, accessories, and cigar related issues. Rocco Barocco brand was added in 1996, they have five locations. Their marketing strategy is to go to the customers. For Furla Boutique, they have two main locations in Kuwait city; they represent 30 % of the local market share for the same category, they use pure genuine leather only, mainly calf skin. Prices range from $300 to $1000. Their weakness is that they have no website. They advertise through al Qabas newspapers and Passions monthly magazine (Kotler and Keller, 2009).

III) - Al Ostoura Company established in 1985. They have eight locations. A limited clothes company, they sell international brands; Emilio Pucci, Moschino, and Francisco Biasia which has been added in 2006. Fransisco Biasia is a pure genuine leather handbags brand, and its prices range between $ 450 and $1200. As per their customer service manager, interviewed through the telephone by Sonia in October 2009, they represent about 30 % of the local market share for the same category, they have their own monthly magazine, and website, in addition to the newspaper advertisements they do regularly three to four times per year, usually during the special occasions as well as when they receive the new collections, or in the case of a sale (Kotler and Keller, 2009).

IV) - The indirect competitors are considered in this dissertation due to the special local culture. A customer may pay $ 4,000 for a Hermes handbag, while she is not willing to pay $ 300 for a non-designer handbag. Most Sonia Amer brand's customers are buying the imitation Gucci, Louis Vuitton and the Hermes with very comparative prices. Under the same market study, Sonia chose two interviewees from the indirect competitors. First was the sales person of the Comfort Shoe, whom she met face to face and asked him the same standard questions asked to the direct competitors. Furthermore Sonia had a phone interview/conversation with the purchasing manager of the Steps Company. Both the sales manager and the purchasing manager mentioned a change in the local market in the late nineties. Kuwaiti society divided into two categories, high and low class, which means there is no more middle level who would be concerned about loyalty. That situation led the Steps Company to close one of its luxury shops due to the high prices which caused a loss, and stick to the low price, low quality with the prices ranging between $ 10 and $ 50 per a handbag or pair of shoes, which is more acceptable to the customers. While it led the Comfort Shoe to increase its prices to the range of $600 to $2000 per handbag, to keep the few high level customers they have, through focusing on European designs and designer names (Kotler and Keller, 2009). Keep in mind that both companies were established in the late eighties (Appendix. 6).

V) - The Intermediates were another avenue to explore. Sonia thought about collaborating with Golden Galaxy Clothes Company, a limited company established in 1990.

Information as per their sales manager interviewed by Sonia on the 25th of March 2009, financially category 1- 10 million USD, they have Italian and French brands such as Zapa, Dusk, Coterie, their prices range between $200 and $2000. However, the deal with Galaxy failed, and a detailed analysis to all the data collected from Sonia Amer trademark documentation has been presented in her dissertation in the following data analysis (Kotler and Keller, 2009).

VI) Complementary business, Sonia interviewed the deputy general manager of Al Babtain library on the 31st of December 2009, to learn from Al Babtain, any experiences in complementary business opportunities and for sponsoring all the literature activities related to the women's rights and creativity (Kotler and Keller, 2009).

CHAPTER 6

Data Analysis

The themes and patterns were the writer of this dissertation's choice for analyzing the data collected. As per Aronson (1994) the first step in the thematic analysis is collecting the data in patterns, while, Aronson (1994) argued that the next step to a thematic analysis is to determine all collected data that relate to the already identified patterns. The thematic method has been used to facilitate understanding the aim and to reach the objective of the dissertation by merging the important themes and patterns in the data collected as stated by Taylor and Bogdan (1984).

Since the themes and patterns were used according to Taylor and Bogdan (1984) to facilitate understanding the aim of the dissertation, by merging the important themes and patterns in the data, the research results can be obtained. The research analysis went in parallel with the data collection (William and Veal, 2000). According to the documents provided by Sonia Amer trademark management, and Gartner's themes of Entrepreneurship. The writer of the study compared the actual activity to the same activity mentioned in the business plan to figure out the mistakes made while implementing the plan. For improving ownership feeling, the writer discusses continually the business progress with the team in one to one meetings with the consultant, the Egyptian and Lebanese operation managers and the sales managers. This discussion is considered a step forward in the study transparency, as a way of getting another opinion. To summarize the data collected in order to analyze it, the writer patterned the subjects as per the following table: the analysis went through two steps; step one within two themes, internal and external situation, step two, the data analysis according to the Gartner's theme adopted in the dissertation.

6.1) The First Step: Each audited situation includes its elements and the way the obstacles were solved. The internal means controlled by the management, the external is out of the management's hands.

6.1.1) Table 4: Data Analysis, the patterns and themes used in analyzing the information collected, resource, Sonia Amer trade mark's documentation, the audit conducted, November, 2011.

Theme	Elements	Problems found	Problems Solving
Internal Situation			
1	Budget and control	Financing	Funding support and Cut cost
		Manufacturing	Improving finishing
2	The marketing strategy	Positioning planning	Changed targeted customers
		Places and locations	Temporary exhibitions
		Pricing strategy	Decreased prices
		High competition	Designs uniqueness
		Brand resistance	Increased awareness
		Customer unsatisfactory	Continual improvement
3	Creating the organization	Part time employees	Commissions
4	Creating value	Lacking of awareness	Literature support
5	Intellectual property strategy	Trademark	Registered
		Copyright	Maintained
External Situation			
1	Special Kuwaiti Culture	Special designs	Introducing new designs
2	Lacking of e-business Culture	Lacking of trust	Fulfill commitments
3	Worldwide Crisis	The Market Fall	Reduced prices by 30 %
4	The Egyptian Revolution	Factory temporary closed	Found alternatives

6.1.2) Theme One - The Internal Situation:

I) Budget and Control: As we all know, budgeting is not an easy task. In general entrepreneurs suffer to find financers due to the risk taken by financing a new venture. Also, there is a hidden costs of other people' money (Bhide, 1999, p.155). In the case study we are investigating the operation manger financed the project with and initial investment of $103,000, in order to manufacture 500 bags. The financing and operating charge agreed was 20 %, and to pay the financing amount back to him within 6 months. A high manufacturing price was noticed; the reason is the high numbers of models and designs wanted and the little quantity required. There were 10 designs, 50 pieces of each design, in three colors. Furthermore, finishing problems appeared due to the shortage of time given to the factory. Sonia solved the Budget and Control Obstacles by:

A) Getting funding support from the factory and the financer, 10 % discount has been made for the total amount paid - 5 % from the factory side and 5% from the financing side. That support allowed Sonia to save an amount of $10,000. Also she got a more payment flexible schedule.

B) Manufacturing wise, the last five new designs had not been manufactured, just marketed as per order option. Also, Sonia shifted to cheaper leathers starting with the three new designs by using sheep and goat leather, in order to increase the margin. For customer satisfaction, the factory improved the finishing. The sales revenue improved so that on the 13th of April 2011, it was $34, 200, including Lebanon sales, and the net profit was $1,500.

C) Cutting cost came as a reflection on the lack of cash the brand faced in November 2009, the expected cash flow was $28,000, while the business growth expected between 18 % for 2011 (Stancil, 1997). The cutting cost implemented through avoiding permanent rent by attending temporary exhibitions. A number of brochures were printed with a cost of $300, and were distributed during the exhibitions to pass the message to the customers, families and friends. Some customers reserved some items with a down payment of $ 15 - $30, not refundable. Also she displayed her handbags in some handbags shops, but only two bags sold in six months due to the high price in comparison to the shops' products.

II) Marketing Strategy: While investigating the writer of this dissertation found that the planned brand positioning was wrong. The brand is far from the targeted customers:

A - The Leather Palace, price range is from $ 300- $ 750 and they have nine locations.

B - Al Sawani Center, price range is from $ 300 - $ 1000, and they have five locations.

C - Al Ostoura Co, price range is from $ 450 - $ 1200, and they have eight locations.

D - Sonia Amer price range is from $ 150 - $ 600, and they have two locations.

The Target- Customer Segments are:

1) Age segment 20- 60 year old Kuwaiti Women, 60 % of their target, design and quality conscious.

2) Age segment 15- 20 year old Kuwaiti women, 30 % of their target, price and design conscious.

customers is higher. The rent cost in the old traditional malls is acceptable, but it has less customers. Furthermore, the lower economic class customers are not willing to pay a higher price for a handbag. In addition, the show room in old malls will affect the brand image as it means going into low profile marketing. Beit Lothan Exhibition was considered a main location target in Sonia's plan due to its good reputation, and customer level, but the exhibition was allocated for traditional products display only as it is a cultural place and therefore it cannot be used for displaying commercial products. That is how Beit Deva, a well known touristic exhibition, became the only displaying place for Sonia's products. Then, Flamingo was rented. It is the first permanent exhibition rented by the brand with an amount of $ 1,000 per month, effective 1st of April 2011. A new show room owned by Sonia's husband in Lebanon will be used as a permanent show room for the brand in Lebanon, starting June 2012.

C) Pricing strategy, the low price strategy failed due to the high manufacturing and funding costs. The suggested 50% margin is considered very low; for the brand to survive the margin should be at least 150 % to cover the fixed, variable, direct and indirect expenses, especially in such expensive rent countries such as Kuwait and Lebanon (Eddie and Maclaney, 2009). The low price strategy increased the customer database, but with a negative impact on the income statement. The pricing strategy has been reviewed, according to the first year of operation, a 30 % discount has been implemented, and the customers target segmentation has been adjusted to focus more on lower was very high and customer impression was noticed. But, an unnecessarily large quantity of the paper bags has been printed. Eezeeclick, a commercial website, was the first online appearance for the brand under a one year agreement. The agreement result was only one call received from a wholesale company. Furthermore, the website of Sonia Amer brand, which was established in March 2010, doesn't include the online payment ability and it faces some resistance. Despite fulfilling commitments, some regional cultural resistance is there (Turban *et al.*, 2010). Another obstacle appeared because the Gulf Web company, which is handling the web design, doesn't offer the on line payment service. So far, the brand account details are sent to the customers in the case of ordering the handbag. Some customers are not confident transferring money to the brand's account. Also, the high cost of shipping is considered another big barrier for international customers, despite the agreement with FedEx for the best possible package. Only two orders have been received through the website. However, the website www.soniaamer.com has been enriched with a clear selling policy, it is the first official e- shop for the brand, well built and continually updated with the new models and designs. The first campaign covered 80,000 work and personal e-mails inside Kuwait, it included employees mixed of men and women, the list provided by the Gulf Web Company. Moreover, a facebook group has been established connected to the web site, the clicks reached 4,190 by the 1st of November 2011. The website and the facebook group are advertised by the personal facebook page of Sonia, Linked In, E Marketing Association, Saudi Arabia Marketing Association and many other groups. Mobile messages are sent to customers for each Eid greeting and exhibition.

III) Creating the Organization: Organizational infrastructure requests delegating tasks, specializing tasks, mobilizing funds for growth and creating a track record (Bhide, 1999, p. 28). The investigation showed that tasks were delegated, but the team is not dedicating full time to the brand marketing, the local distributors showed less commitment than expected, and the international channels are very limited due to the brand resistance. Sonia's full time job negatively affected the speed of the marketing process and opportunities to attend exhibitions, while the shortage of cash caused the lack of a well-trained sales manager to handle the sales and marketing. Ten sales ladies were contacted to be the brand distributors in Kuwait, a discounted price given to them, to add the margin they can get. This strategy has been adapted because the customers were not from the same level. However, the local distributors were not able to sell due to the high prices they requested. Sonia marketed her brand in the ladies gatherings. An Iranian lady appreciated the work and suggested to export the brand to Tehran. Through LinkedIn, and its related groups, E- Marketing Association, Saudi Arabia Business and Professional Network, Jobs in Lebanon, University of Wales and Sonia Amer group, distributors appeared in Romania, Holland, Abu Dhabi, Algeria, and Saudi Arabia. Pink Moon online boutique and Souq.com are channels of marketing that have been approached by the management, but no agreements have been finalized yet.

Finally, the audit conducted showed that there were no written policies and procedures except the sales policy mentioned on the website, and no employment agreements signed with the key persons.

IV) Creating Value: Sonia specified her business mission by caring about more than money (Luke, 2006). Taking the example of Al Babtain library, Al Babtain was founded to encourage the formal traditional poem construction at the same time to support the business of Mr. Abdul Aziz Al Babtain, the businessman and the poet. And according to the cause of Sonia Amer's brand, which is supporting the Arabic literature, Sonia entered the world of the well-known writers in the Arabic world. To be part of them she started publishing her stories and poems, in order to support the handbags business. A facebook page as a newsletter for her literature work opened, the number of friends succeeded 1100 in October 2011, and she started publishing her TV and Radio interviews on the page; then people started recognizing her handbags.

V) The Intellectual Property Strategy: Sonia certified the business, the category of 18-25, designer manufacturer and distributor of genuine leather products, registered under the number 123196 and 123197 Certificates in 2009, Beirut, Lebanon. The period of validity is 15 years - expiration date is 2024, able to be renewed. "A trade mark is a sign that is used to distinguish the goods or services offered by one undertaking from these offered by another; the trademark should be functional, distinctive and not descriptive. It is different than the service mark. The service mark is similar to trademark, differing only in that the latter protects, while the former protects services. Generally speaking, the term trademark includes both trademark and service mark" (©WIPO/OMPI pp. 3-4).

The trade secrets are protected under the copyright law since the copyright is concerned with protecting the work of the human intellects (©WIPO/OMPI). The leaflets, banners and fliers are a part of the copyright, too. The related rights are also protected "They are not copying rights, but they are closely associated with it, they are derived from a work protected by the copyright" (©WIPO/OMPI, p.2). Therefore, if the essential copyright owner is Sonia Amer ™, the related rights become owned by the brand. For example, if any other designer sold his design to the brand, the design will be the brand's copyright (©WIPO/OMPI). Still a written agreement should be there specifying the rights and obligations of both the designer and the brand. The agreement should be completed through a legal firm or through the brand lawyer, in order to avoid infringement and imitating from the company side.

The customer database, procedures, annual reports, code of conduct, and knowhow are all under the umbrella of the trade secrets. They are considered confidential unless the brand becomes a corporate/public company. This confidential information is protected by the national civil law too, and the employees should sign confidentiality agreements or it could be mentioned as a defined clause in the employment agreement itself. In the case of violation, civil punishment could be taken by a local court against the violating person whom violated the policies and procedures (©WIPO/OMPI).

The exclusive domain name has been reserved under the Gulf web company registration certificate; it has been done under a clear signed agreement between the brand and the Gulf web company. The company ensured that they are not duplicating or infringing others' rights. As per the Berne Convention, the automation processes are protected by the copyright law without any official registration as long as it is mentioned on the written information, copyright and the year of production, all rights reserved Sonia Amer trade mark (©WIPO/OMPI). The domain name (soniaamer. com), the logo, the trademark name, the slogan, the music, the photos, the videos, and the screen display (WIPO/OMPI, pp. 7, 17, 35).

Furthermore, Sonia implemented the IP strategy. The IP (Intellectual Property) has been handled seriously locally, but not internationally due to the high expenses required to register the brand in each and every country. IP auditing has been done as the first step of the internal strategy "It is a systematic review of the IP assets owned, used or acquired by a business. Its purpose is to uncover under- utilized IP assets, to identify any threats to a company's bottom line, to enable business planners to devise informed strategies that will maintain and improve the company's market position" (©WIPO/OMPI, pp. 1-5). An IP culture started being implemented within the brand to enhance values. An IP strategy has been adopted for better positioning and development capability, such as defining the kind of thinking the brand needs to survive and become international.

6.1.3) Theme Two, the External Situation: The external situation is summarized as following:

I) The Special Kuwaiti Culture, The traditional Kuwaiti women's dress is the Aabaya (a long black dress to cover the lady's body). Fashion wise, the local ladies' main focus is the handbags, since they are the only things that can be shown. The Kuwaiti society is divided into Bedouin and Urban. The Bedouin ladies care about designs and colors more than quality. Furthermore, the main customers are Bedouins. Their shopping habits are cost sensitive and stereotypical. The accepted price range for them is $ 50 to $120 per handbag, unless it is the original brand name (Eddie and Maclaney, 2009). Urban customers are more into genuine products and they are willing to pay the double or triple the price if they feel the piece is worth it, but they are very selective and they prefer brand names.

II) Lack of e-Business Culture: Although Sonia showed honesty and commitment fulfillment to online customers, customs barriers appeared which caused some dissatisfaction to an international customer in Africa. The e-commerce practice in the Arab World is still very limited. The Middle Eastern countries are still suffering from the lack of trust and honesty in the International market. For example, the e-marketing campaign arranged by the Gulf web company; the e- mail message reached 80,000 customers, generated only two calls, even though both customers asked to see the products before making the decision to buy (Appendix 7).

III) Worldwide Crisis and Market Fall, In June 2009, when Sonia conducted the market research, the Kuwaiti market showed a range of sale of 30 to 40 bags per month in Furla shop, while 10 to15 Cromina or Pontatras in the Leather

Palace and 15 to 20 bags in Francisco Biasia. Furthermore, while doing the market research the price range of a genuine handbag was from $50 - $ 600 at the direct competitors' show rooms. While, when Sonia Amer ™ started operating in September 2009, the market had already fallen and 5 to 10 bags became the new range of handbags sold per month. The number of new designs has been reduced and the price range had dramatically reduced.

IV) The Egyptian Revolution: As a result of the Egyptian revolution started on 25th of January 2011, the factory was closed for quite a long time, which led Sonia to search for alternate locations, such as Syria, Morocco, Lebanon and Turkey. The alternatives created concerns about manufacturing, leather source of origin and overhead cost (Appendix 8).

6.2) The second step: The data analysis according to Gartner's themes have been summarized as per the following:

6.2.1) Entrepreneur, involves individuals with unique personality characteristic and abilities (Gartner, 1990). Sonia is a stubborn risk taker and decision maker. At the same time she is more experienced in auditing a business, then operating it.

6.2.2) Innovation, doing something new as an idea, product, service, market or technology in a new or established organization (Gartner, 1990). Innovation is not really extraordinary in Sonia Amer trademark case study; the main innovations are in the bags' designs.

6.2.3) Organization creative, describes the behaviors involved in creating organizations (Gartner, 1990). The case study showed a group of friends and family members are supporting an ambitious entrepreneur to succeed in her very risky venture. The members of the team do not know each other, and they do not work in harmony, each member was isolated, struggling to finish the task Sonia required from his/her side.

6.2.4) Creating value is the idea that entrepreneurship creates value (Gartner, 1990). The information collected from the case study showed that the only value created is encouraging the Arabic literature by linking the literature to the product.

6.2.5) Organization profit or not profit, concerns whether entrepreneurship involves profit making only (Garner, 1990). The first reason Sonia established her business is earning money, she needed to increase her income, when she felt that jobs are not secured, the cause she created to her business is supporting the Arabic literature and the women's rights.

6.2.6) Uniqueness, entrepreneurship involves uniqueness (Gartner, 1990). Sonia's products are unique, special designs with special leather, they need to keep improving designs and finishing.

6.2.7) Owner manager, entrepreneurship reinforces the involvement of individuals who are owners and managers of their own business (Gartner, 1990). That was very clear in the case study; Sonia is an example of a committed and a hard worker.

At the end of this chapter the writer of the study confirms the validity of the information by involving the shareholders (Gillham, 2000).

According to the data collected and analyzed, the writer finalized the findings as per the following chapter.

CHAPTER 7

Findings

According to the objective of this dissertation, which is helping the entrepreneurs to avoid start-up obstacles and in order to answer the research question defining the limitations of the entrepreneur's role in implementation of an entrepreneurship while creating an organization, the writer of this dissertation classified the findings according to the subjects audited in the case study selected. Each activity has been audited and the non-conformities finalization based on the approved business plan provided. The business plan has been treated as the lone official documented policies and procedures, in addition to the selling policy available on the website.

The evaluation percentage of the entrepreneurship implementation effectiveness was based on Gartner's themes of entrepreneurship (1990), which has been adapted and used as a framework and a foundation for answering the research question. Step one; the writer provided a full explanation how the findings have been finalized. Step two; the writer used Gartner's themes of entrepreneurship as a base and a bench mark for the evaluation.

7.1) Step One; a detailed explanation to the finalized findings.

7.1.1) Table 5: Audit Findings, resource, Sonia Amer trademark's documentation, the audit conducted, November, 2011.

Elements	Problems found	Problems Solving	Finding
Internal Situation			
Budget and control	Financing Manufacturing	Funding support and Cut cost Improving finishing	Support was not continual and cutting cost hearted the brand image There was no criteria for improvement
The marketing strategy	Positioning planning Places and locations Pricing strategy High competition Brand resistance Customer unsatisfactory	Changed targeted customers Temporary exhibitions Decreased prices Designs uniqueness Increased awareness Continual improvement	Shifting to low class customers changed the brand positioning The show room was required for branding and recognizing Decreasing prices leads to loss No bench mark for uniqueness Higher awareness required The targeted customers already changed
Creating the organization	Part time employees	Commissions	Policies and procedures, salary scale, risk and reward were missing
Creating value	Lacking of awareness	Literature support	An overlap between the value of the product or the entrepreneur behavior
Intellectual property strategy	Trademark Copyright	Registered Maintained	The international registration also needed for avoiding imitating
External Situation			
Special Kuwaiti Culture	Special designs	Introducing new designs	Targeted customers should be specified
Lacking of e-business Culture	Lacking of trust	Fulfill commitments	On line payment was highly required for activating shopping
Worldwide Crisis	The Market Fall	Reduced prices by 30%	Reducing prices hearted the brand image
The Egyptian Revolution	Factory temporary closed	Found alternatives	Turkey as a source of origin was a clear violence against the policy

According to the findings table, the writer of the dissertation can say that;

7.1.2) The budget and control; the budget and control were not well planned. A list of alternatives were not available in the documents audited, such as the banks debits probabilities, the interest rates provided, the payment conditions, etc. The financial support of deducting 10% from the whole amount received from the operation manager and the factory was not enough to cover the cash problem the brand faced due to the lack of sales (Eddie and Maclaney, 2009). The audit conducted showed that Sonia went into the basket of investment varieties: in the balance sheet, under the non-current asset some of Sonia's properties were mentioned such as the car, the land and the shares as alternatives and as a backup plan in case of cash shortage (Appendix 3). That shows the high risk Sonia took to start her business, she dedicated all her properties, and the 120,000-dollar investment is considered very high compared to Sonia's financial liquidity situation. What entrepreneurs should know is that "Entrepreneurs must reconcile what they want with what they are willing to risk" (Bhide, 1999, p.8).

7.1.3) Wrong IP strategy; the audit also highlighted a duplicated cost through the registration of two logos, the signature and the elephant. While the SA logo is still not registered, it is protected by the copyright. Ensuring international registration validity in "Madrid systems for trademarks" according to the WIPO "World Intellectual Property Organization" is required, for avoiding imitations, a Chinese company already tried to register the same brand name in china's chamber of commerce. The large quantity of bags manufactured without insuring the channels of sales was a problem. The 2009 income statement included the whole amount of expenses such as the designs samples, the stationary, the registration certificates in addition to the travel expenses. That amount has been deducted from 2009 sales revenue only, instead of dividing the amount from the number of the items (handbags, purses and accessories), in order to be added to the mark up.

7.1.4) Manufacturing; the problems were investigated by merging the important themes and patterns in the data provided (Taylor and Bogdan, 1984). Some obvious improvements were made in the last three models manufactured in 2010, compared to the previous models, which included some finishing problems, such as the skin smell, and the loose bottoms. Even so, the sales results of the three new models were not encouraging. Furthermore, the criteria of best quality or better quality was not clearly specified; some specifications were available such as the kind of skin used, the color and size required, no bench mark for product acceptance was available, the production process performance was missing and there was no clear agreement with the factory defining the terms and conditions. Finally, the problems started in Egypt in January 2011 caused a delay of receiving the samples of the 2012 collection and Syria is no longer an alternative option due to the latest revolution situation. Other Arabic alternatives such as Morocco or Lebanon are suitable solutions, but Turkey as a source of origin is a policy violation against the (Pure Arabic product) concept.

7.1.5) Marketing-wise; the writer of the dissertation used the KPI's (Key Performance Indicators) as a tool of measurement for each campaign such as the number of delivered messages by the campaign, audience exposed, audience targeted, and number of customers gained according to the campaign (Kotler and Keller, 2009). The ISO (9001- 2008) standards were in use for the performance measurements. Likewise, according to Brown (2006, p.14) the writer used the SWOT Analysis, (Strength, Weaknesses, Opportunities and Threats) as another tool for the performance measurement:

I) Strengths; The Lebanese brand is accepted by the Kuwaiti customers, high quality leather is used, special designs, acceptable prices, good connections, expansion plans through e-marketing channels, associations, organizations and individuals, no tax barriers, Kuwait – Cairo- Beirut "tax free, due to some agreements", certified suppliers, well known factory in Egypt. For successful public relations they have a good relationship with the Arabic journalists and TV programmers; it is the insider's way to get successful media coverage (Dunn, 2005).

II) Weaknesses; The brand is local, Egyptian made is not as trusted in terms of finishing, Lebanon has a tax of 10 % which would increase the markup. Also, shifting to a lower class means changing the targeted customers. However, the provided positioning plan showed a great gap between the brand and its targeted customers, due to the low price strategy Sonia adopted when she started the business. In addition, the wrong kick off timing (the last week of Ramadan) the swine flu, return from summer vacations and back to school season also had an effect.

III) Opportunities; According to the strength and weakness noticed two choices are suggested, either increase the prices to be even with the highest brand competitors and invest in a better finishing and unique designs, a presentable permanent show room, in addition to aggressive marketing campaigns to increase the awareness, or change the whole scenario, including the competitors, in which case the Chinese products will be the main marketing barrier due to the lowest prices provided. The benchmark and the criteria based on for specifying the competitors were not mentioned in the data collected. Other connection channels such as my space and blogs have been created, but are not really active due Sonia's lack of time. A proposal with $ 15,000 expenses has been received from the Lebanese marketing company, Mazaya, which suggested marketing the brand in the gulf area within six months. The proposal has been postponed due to the lack of cash and the insufficient marketing suggestions provided.

IV) Threats; Regarding the main threat - the competitors, the competition criteria looked insufficient. The list of competitors mentioned in the business plan is not logical to some extent according to the competitors' long history in the market, their international brand names, their number of locations, their unique designs, their high price range, their organizations' volume, and their number of employees. Even though, Furla, Cromina and Pontatras' prices have been reduced dramatically, responding to the market fall while Sonia kept her prices low, they were still considered expensive by her customers. Eventually, the investigation showed that the high competition to Sonia's products appeared from the Chinese made products, the imitated brand names such as Louis Vuitton, Channel, Chloe and others. The prices of those imitated products are within the same range of Sonia's prices, the places they are sold are exhibitions, and the customers are the same.

7.1.6) The questionnaire results; The writer of this report considered the customer survey results unsatisfactory, as per the ISO (9001- 2008) standards of measuring continual improvement. The writer used ISO as a sample for the performance measurement tool due to her experience as a quality assurance manager; she is a certified auditor by Lloyd company. The measurements are the risk and rewards on an activity based management, product data management, employee involvement, integrated change management, certified suppliers, preventive action boards, total productive maintenance, and a corporate thinking strategy would be able to create new knowledge (ISO 9001- 2008). The results of the survey were accordingly 68 % found the product 'trendy'. 66 % found the price 'reasonable'. 56 % found the quality 'very good'. 88 % answered the collection varieties could be used both 'casual and for evenings'. 95 % knew about the brand 'through a friend'. 66 % would 'recommend it' to their friends. So as an approximate overall satisfaction percentage we have 73 % (68+ 66+ 56+ 88+ 95+ 66 = 439 /6= 73,16), which is considered very low for the management satisfaction, requiring at least 85 %. According to those results, quality, customer service, creative capability and competitive cost position, balanced scorecards for a vision and strategy such as financial, customers, earning and growth, internal business processes, objective measures, target and initiatives were not fruitfully met (Eddie and Maclaney, 2009). Other surveys are required after three to six months or after marketing new designs, to obtain new feedback and compare it to the previous, in addition to taking into consideration the new level of the customers targeted.

7.1.7) The interviews conducted; Regarding the interviews conducted, eight interviews were found because Sonia conducted two structured interviews in Al Oustoura, the sales person in Fransisco Biasia show room and the service manager of Al Ostoura Co. That is how the structured interviews were seven and one more semi structured interview with Al Babtain deputy general manager has been conducted. At the same time, the interviews were not recorded on a CD or cassette tape, nor were the documented questions and answers signed by the interviewees.

7.1.8) The research methodologies have been implemented, primary and secondary data collected, quantitative and qualitative collecting data methods used such as questionnaires and interviews to ensure credibility. Themes and patterns data analysing samples have been also used for the report validity. The KPI's, SWOT analysis and ISO (9001- 2008) standards used as measurement tools, to measure the effectiveness and continual improvement for each activity. In addition to the brand provided documentation, the books, journals, magazines and studying materials, internet research also used for enriching the dissertation with the previous literature review on the same subjects, and providing the dissertation an academic value.

7.2) Step two; after highlighting the findings, Gartner's entrepreneurship themes were used as a base and a bench mark for subjective evaluation, each theme to each activity as following:

7.2.1) Entrepreneur, Entrepreneurship involves individuals with unique personality characteristic and abilities (Gartner, 1990). Sonia planned to adopt the 'contribute and commitment' leadership style, while she implemented the one man show style (McKee and Carlsosn, 1999). Sonia's husband, the business consultant, mentioned that she "threw a bomb between our feet and asked us to stay alive". She is really stubborn. Her brother, the operation manger for Lebanon, said Sonia was not listening to anyone; no one was allowed to ask questions and receive correct and standardized information (Robins and Timothy, 2008).

7.2.2) Innovation: Doing something new as an idea, product, service, market or technology in a new or established organization (Gartner, 1990). The two innovations Sonia employed are providing a purely Arabic product and relating the handbags to the literature with her suggested slogan 'the only bag with a poem.

7.2.3) Organization Creation: Describes the behaviors involved in creating organizations (Gartner, 1990). The written policies and procedures were not mentioned anywhere except the business plan, and the online selling policy. Although the team was created, there were no employment agreements signed, or codes of conduct.

7.2.4) Creating values: Entrepreneurship creates value (Gartner, 1990). An overlap between the value of the product provided and the value of the entrepreneur behavior was noticed during the investigation. Is the venture about both Sonia the writer and Sonia the designer or about Sonia Amer genuine leather handbags brand?.

7.2.5) Profit and Non- Profit: Concerns whether entrepreneurship involves profit making only (Gartner, 1990). It is a profit business for a cause, which is supporting Arabic literature.

7.2.6) Growth: The importance of growth as a characteristic of entrepreneurship (Gartner, 1990). Expansion was mentioned in the business plan has started already within the new show room in Lebanon.

7.2.7) Uniqueness: Entrepreneurship involves uniqueness. Uniqueness is a main requirement for being entrepreneurs (Gartner, 1990). This theme should be linked to the creating value; actually it includes both the uniqueness of the product and the entrepreneur. The uniqueness of the business is the pure Arabic product concept, while the uniqueness of Sonia is the combination between being a writer and a designer.

7.2.8) The Owner – Manager: Entrepreneurship involves individuals who are owners and manager of their business (Gartner, 1990). Despite her committed involvement and dedication, Sonia over managed her own business. While, all that ventures need is a smooth combination of innovation and control.

Findings

At the end of this chapter the writer of this dissertation can say that the objective of the dissertation has been met by explaining the difference between entrepreneur and entrepreneurship. Although we cannot split the dancer from the dance, the entrepreneur is the dynamo of the entrepreneurship, while creating the organization only (Gartner, 1988). The dissertation explained the limitations of the entrepreneur's role in implementing entrepreneurship, while creating the organization, due to many other important elements. It is a set of activities involved in organization creation, the organizations also behave (Robins and Timothy, 2008). As mentioned earlier in the literature review, the entrepreneurs are individuals with unique personality characteristics and abilities, while entrepreneurship is the creation of new organizations (Gartner, 1990). So we need to change the "Who is the entrepreneur?" question to "what is the entrepreneurship about?" (Gartner (1998, pp.11-31). As per the literature review, the trait approach which considered the entrepreneur to have a set of personality traits and characteristics has been considered unfruitful, while the behavioral approach which prefers the set of activities involved in creation of the organization has been considered a better approach to be adopted by the new created organizations. In the entrepreneurship behavioral approach, an entrepreneur is a set of activities involved in the organization creation. Also, behavioral approach has been considered more productive for research in entrepreneurship (Gartner, 1988).

However, by the end of this chapter, we can assure that all the new ventures need a smooth combination

CHAPTER 8

Conclusions and Implications

As discussed earlier in this dissertation, although it is difficult to tell the dancer from the dance, and to differentiate between entrepreneurship and the entrepreneur, to be an entrepreneur, you need more then taking the financial risk and providing a new service or a product in a well prepared portfolio business plan (Gartner, 1988). Good managers need to be good decision makers, good communicators, good listeners, distribute authority, share information, adapt change, be flexible and support innovation and continual development (Robins and Timothy, 2008). That is how some new ventures succeed while others fail. And that is how more questions come to our mind such as; what are the essential elements of entrepreneurship? How can we become successful entrepreneurs and why? How can entrepreneurs make right decisions? What kinds of markets and internal environments foster the most successful entrepreneurial activities? (Amit *et al*. 2007). The writer of this dissertation ensures that, the organization needs to behave too, and that behavior requires a set of activities involved in organization creation. Funding, plans and strategies, the people involved, the internal and external customers (internal customers are the employees; the external customers are the regular customers), the suppliers and the competitors, continual audit and development. Also one must consider the internal environment, including the written policies and procedures because at top companies, the metrics help to identify the potential leaders and develop their skills (Robert and Robin, 2008). Similarly, the auditing policy, the corporate culture, the risk and reward system are essential for company success, as well as the ethics and ownership feeling by allowing employees to ask questions and getting constructive information. Otherwise, good employees will leave for better opportunities. When good people sometimes say yes to bad and unethical or illegal actions, there are four possible reasons: the organization's values are fuzzy to them, those unclear values lead the good employees to less developing intuition and expedient criteria, they may not be clear on their own values or their interpretation of probability leads them to think that their hands are tied, and conveniently favors their prior preferred option. They have no other options. Such a situation needs a direct addressing of ethical decision-making in the organizations by the senior management (MIT Sloan Management Review, Summer, 2008).

The dissertation confirmed the literature reviews mentioned earlier, with a life sample, a recent entrepreneurship experience. This dissertation is based on qualitative and quantitative collecting data approaches. It is one case study, with a deep and focused analysis for explanation and academic benefits. The implication of this dissertation is that it is a one case study about the writer of the dissertation's own business. In other words, it is an example of a self-criticism for a small business by the writer. Similar cases were not found in previous research. In previous research, the case study taken is mainly some other's venture audited by one researcher or a group of researchers. What gives the validity of this dissertation is that the NCR's (Non Conformity Reports) conducted by Sonia as is an auditor are documented and available in the trademark documentation (Appendix 9). The audit conducted was subjective (audit per subject) and at the same time objective (Continual improvement), and measurable (ISO, February 22, 2011). Moreover, the documented and approved business plan used as policies and procedures, and Gartner's themes of entrepreneurship framework was the benchmark, and the utilization of multi collection data approaches supported the transparency in addition to the use of themes and patterns analyzing sample and the use of performance measurements.

Finally, we can assure that all the new ventures need a smooth combination of innovation and control. The entrepreneur has limits, market studies, marketing strategies, legal issues, funding, technology, manufacturing should be handled by specialties, entrepreneur should delegate tasks and follow up to get the jobs done in a coherent way. In addition to the external circumstances which may negatively affect the business progress, the entrepreneur cannot handle them. All what entrepreneur can do is to be flexible enough to adapt to change and adjust the business plans as per the circumstances without hurting the policy. However, the

CHAPTER 9

Limitations and Recommendations

Eventually, the limitation of this dissertation is that it is the writer own business case study. Automatically that decreases its level of credibility due to the improbability of subjective judgment. Writers in general are honest, transparent and they have a large imagination as well. That might lead to either underestimating or overestimating the business results and achievements. That's why it is logical to have another opinion; it is needed. That opinion will take the role of external auditor to approve proposed and to recommend further improvement steps. So, another researcher to investigate the same case study and add his implications is required. Also, a similar case study is required for comparison. Comparison reaches should be similar in the circumstances when the researcher is the owner of the business itself., similarity in the business size and domain, despite the differentiation between entrepreneurs' personalities and skills. Moreover, Sonia used the ISO audit tool for measuring the data validity and conformities according to her experience as an internal auditor, but Sonia Amer brand is not officially ISO certified. Also, the findings did not include the deadlines for correcting nonconformities as per the ISO (9001- 2008) standards. Furthermore, the interviews collected involved sales persons and purchasing managers, it did not involve shareholders, who could be considered more reliable for collecting data. Also, the interviews were not recorded or signed by the interviewees.

The investigation went through the limited information available there are no documents provided by the competitors, such as annual reports. The customers' survey has been collected upon the opening exhibition, while new level of customers has been targeted in a later stage, those customers have not yet provided feedback, and that requires collecting a new survey. The measurement used for performance as well may not be the best; there may be different systems of performance measurement considered more advanced and accurate such as the Six Sigma and the Three Sixty Degree appraising.

However, the dissertation highlighted some of the startup problems that may face any entrepreneur and provided them the best possible explanation within the limited available information. Within a chosen theoretical framework such as Low and MacMillan (1988) it is mentioned that it is time for entrepreneurship researchers to pursue causality more aggressively. Low and MacMillan (1988) stated that the recent trend toward the theories defining the entrepreneurship driven research that is contextual and process oriented is encouraging. At the same time, Low and MacMillan (1988) suggested that the exploratory studies that are not theory driven should be discouraged unless the topic is highly original. Other theories could be a useful tool such as the entrepreneurship themes provided by Deniz *et al.* (2000) covering the Entrepreneurship theory, types of entrepreneurs, the entrepreneurial process, and external environments for entrepreneurship. Keep in mind that "the desire for common definitions and a clearly defined area of inquiry for entrepreneurship" as per Low and MacMillan (1988, p.141) has not yet been met by the researchers. Although the dissertation covered some areas of the entrepreneurship implementation, and highlighted the limitation of the entrepreneur's role in implementing entrepreneurship, while creating the organization, there are still, many areas that could be targeted for future researchers in order to increase their knowledge and business experience, which is the objective of the dissertation. The future research could be; the limitations of the entrepreneur's role in funding new ventures, marketing strategies, creating organizations and adding values, as well as the flexible management and adapting change according to the external circumstances, in such a fast and variable business environment.

Finally, few previous research studies mentioned the importance of intellectual property role within the entrepreneurship implementation, therefore further research about the importance of intellectual property role within the entrepreneurship implementation is also necessary. The value of intangible assets for company culture based on innovation is an area in need of exploration.

References

Printed Sources

1. Amit, R., Glosten, L., and Muller, E. (1993). *Challenges to Theory Development in Entrepreneurship Research.* Journal of Management Studies, Volume 30, Issue 5, September 1993. PP. 815–834,

2. Aronson, J. (1994). *A Pragmatic View of Thematic Analysis,* The Qualitative Report, an On Line Journal Dedicated to Qualitative Research and Critical Inquiry, Volume 2, Number 1, Spring, 1994.
    http://www.nova.edu/ssss/QR/BackIssues/QR2-1/aronson.html
    [Last accessed in October 29, 2011]

3. Audretsch, D.B.(2007). *The Entrepreneurial Society, Publisher*: Oxford University Press, July 7, 2007. USA.

4. Audretsch, D.B., and Thurik, R. (1999), *Innovation, Industry Evolution and Employment*, Published at Cambridge University Press, 1999, UK.

5. Bechard, J. P., and Gregoire, D. (2005). *Entrepreneurship Education, Research Revised: The Case of Higher*

Education, Academy of Management Learning & Education 2005.

6. Best, J and Khan, J. (1989). *Research in Education,* Englewood Cliffs (NJ), Prentice Hall

7. Bhide, A. (1999), *The Questions Every Entrepreneur Must Answer,* Harvard Business Review on Entrepreneurship, P.8, Harvard Business School Press. Boston, MA 02163. PP.1-28.

8. Brown, B.B. (2006), *Developing a Business Plan that Works* (1st ed.). Indian edition 2006. PP.1, 7, 14.

9. Blaxter, L, Hughes, C and Tight, M (1996). *How to Research,* Buckingham, Open University Press.

10. Delamont, S. (1992), *Fieldwork in Educational Settings: Methods, Pitfalls and Perspectives,* London, Falmer.

11. Dunn, J. (2005). *The Insider's Way to Get Successful Media Coverage.* Successful Public Relation (1st ed.), India.

12. Eddie, A., and Maclaney, P. (2009). *Accounting, An Introduction* (4th ed.), Ch.11, P.396, UK.

13. Gartner, W.B. (1990). *What are we talking about when we talk about entrepreneurship?* Journal of Business Venturing. PP.5, 15-28.

14. Gartner, W.B. (1990), *Themes of Entrepreneurship,* Journal of Small Business & Entrepreneurship. Autumn 1998. PP. 27 -39.

15. Gartner, W.B. (1988). *Who is the entrepreneur? Is the wrong question,* American Journal of Small Business, PP. 11- 31.

16. Gartner, W.B. (1988). *Who is the entrepreneur? Is the wrong question.* Journal of Small Business & Entrepreneurship, vl.15.no2, fall 1998.

17. Gillham, B. (2000). *Case Study Research Methods.* Continuum Press, London, 2000. PP 13- 14.

18. Gillham, B. (2000). *The Research Interview.* Continuum Press, London, 2000. Ch. 12-15.

19. Goldstein, A. S. (2005). *Solving Business Problems.* India, 2005. PP. 7- 8.

20. Grant, M.C. (2011). *Who and What is an Entrepreneur.* Harvard Business Review, July 25, 2011. http://blogs.hbr.org/cs/2011/07/who_and_what_is_ an_entrepreneu.html [Last accessed in September 4, 2011]

21. Goldstein, A.S. (2005). *Solving Business Problems.* India, 2005. PP.7-8.

22. Harvard Business Review, *The High – Performance Organization*, July- August 2005.

23. Hox, J.J, and Boeije, H.R (2007), Data Collection Primary versus Secondary, lgitar, No.13,2007. http://igitur-archive.library.uu.nl/fss/2007-1113-200953/hox_05_data%20collection,primary%20versus%20secondary.pdf
[Last accessed in December 15,2011]

24. Hopkins, W.G (2000). *Quantitative Research Design* http://www.sportsci.org/jour/0001/wghdesign.html
[Last accessed in December 15,2011]

25. Carleen, H. (2007). *Seven Habits of Highly Effective Managers*, published on October18, 2007.
http://gigaom.com/2007/10/18/7-habits-of-highly-effective-managers/
[Last accessed in October 29,2011]

26. Johnson, L. (2008). *Go It Alone with Style, Caution and Thrift,* published by FT: April 30, 2008.

27. Kiva Case Study, Stanford Graduate School of Business, Studying Materials, Investment Management course: Unit 10, Page 1.Kiva, Webpage http://www.kiva.org/
[Last accessed in September 13, 2010]

28. Kotler, P., and Keller, K. L. (2009), *Marketing Management*, (13th ed.), USA.

29. Low, M. B. and MacMillan, I.C. (1988). *Entrepreneurship: Past Research and Future Challenge.* Journal of Management, vol. 14, 2: June 1988. PP. 139-161.

30. Luke, A. (2006). *Pick The Brain.* Why It's Not Selfish to Put Yourself First http://www.pickthebrain.com/blog/put-yourself-first/
[Last accessed in March 23, 2011]

31. Macmillan, H., and Tampoe, M. (2009), *Strategic Management,* UK. 2009, Ch.18.

32. Mani, M. (2006), *Thinking Outside the Box in Company Culture.* http://www.realinnovation.com/content/c090525a.asp
[Last accessed in March 22, 2011]

33. Marty, N. (2005). *The Brand Gap, How to Bridge the Distance between Business Strategy and Design*, MBA program, Robert Kennedy Colege, 2009, Marketing Management Course, Studying Materials, Unit 2.

34. Marty, N. (1996). *Liquid People. Smart. Nice and Really Talented*, Critique Magazine launched in1996. http://stuff.liquidagency.com/index.php/people/fullstory/marty_neumeier/
[Last accessed in March 23, 2011]

35. Mckee, R. K. and Carlson, B. (1999). *The Power to Change*, Grid (2005 ed.). USA.

36. Miller, W.C.(1987). *The Creative Edge*, Addison-Wesley.

37. Moss, D., A. (2007). *Putting the Pieces Together,* the Core Concepts of Macroeconomics, Excerpted from a Concise Guide to Macroeconomics: What Managers, Executives, and Students Need to Know" by Harvard Business Press, Boston, Massachusetts, MBA program, Robert Kennedy Colege, 2009, Investment Management course, Studying Materials, Residency Package, P. 2.

38. Patton, M.Q. (2002). *Qualitative Research and Evaluation Methods.* Thousand Oaks, CA. Sage publishing.

39. Robert, G., and Robin, G. (2008), *Corporate Social Responsibility to Win the War for Talent.* MIT SLOAN MANAGEMENT REVIEW, FALL 2008 PP.65- 69 http://web.mit.edu/org/s/smr/PDFs/50116.pdf [Last accessed in January 17, 2009]

40. Robins, S., and Timothy, J. (2008), *Organizational Behavior,* (13th ed.). USA. Ch.17, p.585.

41. Rock, A. (1987). *Strategy vs. Tactics from a Venture Capitalist.* Harvard Business Review on Entrepreneurship. Harvard Business School Press, Boston, MA 02163. P.135.

42. Sahlman, W. A. (1997). *How to Write a Great Business Plan.* Art. 97409. Harvard Business Review. Published in January-February 1997.USA. pp.29-56.

43. Simmons, K. (1998). *The Practical Pathway to Leadership.* Seven Habits of Highly Effective Managers. Copyright © Creating Wealth Limited, 1998-2009.

44. Stake, R.E.(1995), *The Art of Case Study Research.* Beverly Hills, CA: Sage Publishing.

45. Stancil, J.M. (1997). *How Much Money Does Your New Venture Need? Entrepreneurship.* Harvird Business Review, published in July- August 1997. USA. PP.92-106.

46. Staten, J. B. (1998). *Institutional Innovation and the Future*, The Emergency Response & Research Institute, Chicago, IL.

47. Taylor, S. J, and Bogdan, R. (1984). *Introduction to Qualitative Research Methods: The Search for Meanings.* New York: John Wiley & Sons.

48. Turban, Peng, Effraim, King, David, Turban, Deborah, Lee Jae, Liang, Ting, (2010). *Electronic Commerce* (6th ed.). U.S.A. Ch. 12, 13.

49. Ucbasaran, D., Westhead, P., and Wright, M. (2000). *The Focus of Entrepreneurial Research: Contextual and Process Issues, about the Focus of Entrepreneurial Research Contextual and Process Issues.* The Tenth Global Entrepreneurship Conference, March 2000, by the University of Nottingham Institute for Enterprise and Innovation, March 2000.

50. Welfens, P. J.J. (2002). *The New Economy and Economic Growth in Europe and the US.*

51. William, G.T., and Veal, A.J. (2000). *Business Research Methods.* Pearson Education, Frenchs Forest.

52. WIPO Intellectual Property Handbook: Policy, Law & Use (WIPO Publication No. 489 (E)) 2nd ed. (2004). WIPO/OMPI, *Copyright*, P.2.

53. WIPO Intellectual Property Handbook: Policy, Law & Use (WIPO Publication No. 489 (E)) 2nd ed. (2004). WIPO/OMPI, *On- Line Intellectual Property Management*, pp, 7, 17, 35.

54. WIPO Intellectual Property Handbook: Policy, Law & Use (WIPO Publication No. 489 (E)) 2nd ed. (2004). WIPO/OMPI, *Related Rights*, P.3

55. WIPO Intellectual Property Handbook: Policy, Law & Use (WIPO Publication No. 489 (E)) 2nd ed. (2004). WIPO/OMPI, *Strategy for Intellectual Property Management*, PP. 1-5

56. WIPO Intellectual Property Handbook: Policy, Law & Use (WIPO Publication No. 489 (E)) 2nd ed. (2004). WIPO/OMPI, *Trademark,* PP. 3-4

57. Yin, R. (1984). *Case Study Research: Design and Methods.* Beverly Hills, CA: Sage Publishing.

58. Yin, R. (1993). *Applications of case study research*. Beverly Hills, CA: Sage Publishing.

59. Yin, R. (1994). *Case Study Research: Design and Methods* (2nd ed.). Beverly Hills, CA: Sage Publishing.

60. Zahra, S.A., Jennings, D.F., and Kuratko, D. (1999). *Entrepreneurship*.

61. Zaidah, Z. (2007). *Case Study as a Research Method*. Journal Kemanusiaan bil.9. June 2007.

62. Zotan, A.J. and Audretsch, D.B. (1990). *Innovation and Small Firms*. Massachusetts Institute of Technology, MIT Press 1990.

Websites

1. Al Babtain, Abdul Aziz, 'The Foundation Of Abdul Aziz Al Babtain Prize For Poetic Creativity', http://www.albabtainprize.org/default.aspx?pageId=36
[Last accessed in March 22, 2009]

2. http://www.allbusiness.com/management/382098-1.html
[last accessed in September 14,2011]

3. Al- Oustoura Monthly Magazine, http://www.alostouragroup.com/magazines/index.html
[Last accessed in April 24,2011]

4. Arab Women's Solidarity Association, http://www.awsa. be/index.htm
   [Last accessed in April 3, 2011]

5. Arab Women's Solidarity Association Belgium, http:// www.awsa.be/flyer2_quint_zoom.jpg
   [Last accessed on April 13, 2011]

6. http://www.ahelp.org/Evaluation/CDC/Evidence.aspx
   [last accessed in June 8, 2011]

7. Balanced Scorecards Institute
   http://www.balancedscorecard.org/BSCResources/ AbouttheBalancedScorecard/tabid/55/Default.aspx
   [Last accessed October 31,2011]

8. Being a Good Steward: It s About More Than Money, http://mysuperchargedlife.com/blog/being-a-good-steward-its-about-more-than-money/
   [Last accessed in March 23rd, 2011]

9. Building Trade Organization, Difference between margin and markup
   http://www.buildingtrade.org.uk/articles/markup_ or_margin.html
   [Last accessed in May 9, 2011]

10. Eezeeclick.Co, http://www.eezeeclick.com/arabic/ classifieds_category.aspx?Dep_ID=21
    [Last accessed in September 25,2009]

11. Facebook, http://www.facebook.com/home.php
    [Last accessed in February 6, 2011]

12. Facebook, http://www.facebook.com/home.php#!/pages/
    Sonia-AmerTM/150874641070
    [Last accessed in February 6, 2011]

13. Golden Galaxy Company
    http://mintportal.bvdep.com/MintPortal-LJHKFICI
    FIFIFIAI.urk
    [Last accessed in March 22, 2009]

14. http://gulnazahmad.hubpages.com/hub/-Primary-
    and-Secondary-Data
    [Last accessed in December 18, 2011]

15. International Organization for Standardization, http://
    www.iso.com/
    [Last accessed in February 22, 2011]

16. http://invest.yourdictionary.com/
    [Last accessed in October 30,2011]

17. Kuwait General Data', http://www.populstat.info/Asia/
    kuwaitg.htm
    [Last accessed in March 22, 2009]

18. Kuwaitis Women Forum, http://www.q8yat.com/show
    thread.php?t=509929
    [Last accessed in November 1, 2009]

19. Leather Palace Company, http://www.arabo.com
    [Last accessed in March 22, 2009]

20. LinkedIn Group, http://www.linkedin.com/groups?most
    Popular=&gid=2472542
    (Last accessed in February 4, 2010)

21. Mazaya Marketing Company, http://mazayamarketing.
    com/
    [Last accessed in January 4, 2011]

22. MIT Sloan Management Review, http://sloanreview.
    mit.edu/themagazine/articles/2008/summer/
    [Last accessed in January 17, 2009]

23. Pink Moon Boutique
    http://www.pinkmoonboutique.com/contact_us.asp
    [Last Accessed April 13, 2011]

24. Registrar of Lebanese Companies http://www.ccib.org.
    lb/Home/index.aspx
    [Last accessed in February 2, 2011]

25. Robert Kennedy College, http://college.ch/
    [Last Accessed April 13, 2011]

26. http://sloanreview.mit.edu/the-magazine/articles/2008/
    summer/
    [accessed: 6th January 2009]

27. Sonia Amer Brand, http://www.soniaamer.com
    [Last accessed in February 6, 2011]

28. Souq, an on Line Marketplace, http://www.souq.com/
[Last accessed in February 8, 2011]

29. http://www.themoneyalert.com/writeabusinessplan.
html
[Last accessed in September4, 2011]

30. http://www.themoneyalert.com/whatisanentrepreneur.
html
[Last accessed in September4, 2011]

31. West Handbags, The Best Fashion Source For Your
Designer Handbags, http://www.handbagshoe.com/
designer%20handbags/hermes%20handbags.html
[Last accessed in March 22, 2009]

32. http://www.quickmba.com/strategy/swot/
[Last accessed in October 30, 2011]

33. http://www.wisegeek.com/what-is-an-entrepreneur.htm
[Last accessed in September 4, 2011]

34. Women's Forum Kuwait, http://www.kuwaiteya.
com/vb/
[Last accessed in February 3, 2011]

Appendix (1)

<u>Customer Survey</u>

Name:..

Signature & Date:....................................

Contact numbers/ emails:...........................

How do you like the product?

☐ Trendy ☐ Classic ☐ Old fashion

How do you see the price?

☐ Expensive ☐ Reasonable ☐ Cheap

How do you see the quality?

☐ Very good ☐ Good, ☐ Bad

How do you see the collection varieties?

☐ Casual ☐ Evening use ☐ Both wise

How did you know about us?

☐ Friend ☐ Internet ☐ Magazines

Would you recommend it to your friends?

☐ Sure ☐ Maybe ☐ No

Any extra suggestions?

```
┌─────────────────────────────────────┐
│                                     │
│                                     │
│                                     │
│                                     │
```

The Survey Questionnaire format, and the results received:

How do you like the product?

| 28 | Trendy | 6 | Classic | 7 | Old fashion |

How do you see the price?

| 14 | Expensive | 27 | Reasonable | 0 | Cheap |

How do you see the quality?

| 23 | Very Good | 16 | Good | 2 | Bad |

How do you see the collection varieties?

| 4 | Casual | 1 | Evening use | 36 | Both wise |

How did you know about us?

| 39 | Friend | | Internet | | Magazines , Others | 2 |

Would you recommend it to your friends?

| 27 | Sure | 10 | Maybe | 4 | No |

Any extra suggestions?

| More varieties, more locations, as per request |

Appendix (2)

The interviews list of questions conducted by Sonia Amer on 25th of March 2009:

Interviews

Questions Asked:
What is your company's market share?
What is the date of the company establishment?
How many show rooms does your company have?
What ways of marketing does your company do? Why?
What kinds of leather your handbags are made from?
What your handbags prices range?

Interviewees:
Sales persons

Ways of Interviewing:
Face to face
Through the phone

Companies Names:
The Leather Palace
Al Sawani Center
Al Oustoura Co.

Appendix (3)

Sonia Amer planned Income Statement 2009- 2013:

	2009	2010	2011	2012	2013
Sales					
Sales Revenue	$ 27,000/-	$ 150,582/-	$ 225,000/-	$ 300,000/-	$ 370,000/-
Cost of Good "shipment, interest"	($ 13,418/-)	($ 101,582/-)	($ 150,000/-)	($ 210,000/-)	($ 270,000/-)
Gross profit margin	$ 13,582/-	$ 50,000/-	$ 75,000/-	$ 90,000/-	$ 100,000/-
Administration & Legal " registration, lawyer, Logo, customs, and commissions"	($ 3,500/-)	($ 2,000/-)	($5,000/-)	($ 8,000/-)	($ 10,000/-)
General Expenses "traveling tickets and visas, hotels reservation, telephone calls"	($ 3,679/-)	($ 4,000/-)	($ 6,000/-)	($ 7,000/-)	($8,000/-)
Operating costs					
Advertisements	($ 3,500/-)	($10,000/-)	($12,000/-)	($14,000/-)	(16,000/-)
Rent	($ 1,500/-)	($ 12,000)	($ 24,000/-)	($ 26,000/-)	(28,000/-)
Depreciation	($ 60/-)	($ 1000/-)	($ 1,500/-)	($ 2,000/-)	($ 2,500/-)
Interest expense 10 % "included in the cost"	-	-	-	-	-
Operating & Admin Cost	($ 12,239/-)	($ 29,000/-)	($48,500/-)	($57,000/-)	($ 64,500/-)
Income Before Tax	$1,343/-	$ 21,000/-	$ 26,500/-	$ 33,000/-	$ 36,000/-
Tax	$ 800/-	$ 1,000/-	$ 1,100/-	$ 1,200/-	$1,300/-
Net Income	$ 534/-	20,000/-	$ 25,400/-	$ 31,800/-	$ 34,700/-

Sonia Amer Planned Balance Sheet Statement 2009-2013:

	2009	2010	2011	2012	2013
ASSETS					
Cash	$ 100/-	$ 534/-	20,000/-	$ 25,400/-	$ 31,800/-
Account receivables	$ 1,500/-	$ 8,333/-	$ 12,451/-	$ 16,601/-	$ 20,474/-
Inventory	$ 101,582/-	$ 150,000/-	$ 210,000/-	$ 270,000/-	$ 330,000/-
Other assets "shares in some co's"	$ 12,500/-	$ 13,000/-	$ 13,500/-	$ 14,000/-	$ 14,500/-
Total current assets	**$ 142,582**	**$ 172,676/-**	**$ 256,951/-**	**$ 327,101**	**$ 397,974/-**
Total noncurrent assets " car + land"	**$ 38,000/-**	**$ 39,000/-**	**$ 40,000/-**	**$ 41,000/-**	**$ 42,000/-**
Total assets	$ 153,482/-	$ 210,676/-	$ 295,851/-	$ 366,901/-	$ 438,674/-
LIABILITIES					
Account payable	$ 101,582/-	$ 150,000/-	$ 210,000/-	$ 270,000/-	$ 330,000/-
Taxes	& 800/-	$ 1,000/-	$ 1,100/-	$ 1,200/-	$1,300/-
Expenses	$20,000/-	$ 30,000/-	$ 35,000/-	$ 30,000/-	$ 26,000/-
Current portion of long-term debt	$ 18,000/-	$ 15,000/-	$ 20,000/-	$ 21,901	$ 22,674/-
Total current liabilities	**$ 140,382**	**$ 196,000/-**	**$ 266,100/-**	**$ 323,101/-**	**$ 379,974/-**
Total noncurrent liabilities "rent + admin, expansion"	**$ 5,100/-**	**$ 14,676/-**	**$ 29,751/-**	**$ 43,800/-**	**$ 58,700/-**
Total liabilities and capital	$153,482	$ 210,676/-	$ 295,851	$ 366,901/-	$ 438,674/-

Sonia Amer Planned Cash Flow Statement 2009-2013:

	2009	2010	2011	2012	2013
Operating cash inflows					
Cash	$100/-	$ 534/-	20,000/-	$ 25,400/-	$ 31,800/-
Net Sales	$ 27,000/-	$ 150,582/-	$ 225,000/-	$ 300,000/-	$ 370,000/-
Other income	$ 12,500/-	$ 13,000/-	$ 13,500/-	$ 14,000/-	$ 14,500/-
Account receivable	($ 1,500/-)	($ 8,333/-)	($ 12,451/-)	($ 16,601/-)	($ 20,474/-)
Net operating cash inflows	**$ 25,400/-**	**$ 155,783/-**	**$ 276,049/-**	**$ 322,799/-**	**$ 396,300/-**
Operating cash outflows					
Cost of goods sold	($ 13,418/-)	($ 101,582/-)	($ 150,000/-)	($ 210,000/-)	($ 270,000/-)
General & admin	$ 7, 179/-	$ 6,000/-	$ 11,000/-	$ 15,000/-	$ 18,000/-
Selling expense	$ 5,060/-	$ 23,000/-	$ 37,500/-	$ 42,000/-	$ 46,500/-
Taxes	& 800/-	$ 1,000/-	$ 1,100/-	$ 1,200/-	$1,300/-
Inventory	$ 101,582/-	$ 150,000/-	$ 210,000/-	$ 270,000/-	$ 330,000/-
Prepaid expenses	$ 3,000/-	$ 6,000/-	$9,000/-	$ 12,000/-	$ 15,000/-
Account payable	($ 101,582/-)	($ 150,000/-)	($ 210,000/-)	($ 270,000/-)	($ 330,000/-)
Net operation cash outflows	**$ 2,621/-**	**($ 62,582/-)**	**($ 91,400/-)**	**($ 139,800/-)**	**($ 189,200/-)**
Net operation cash flows	$ 28,021/-	$ 93,201/-	$ 184,649/-	$ 182,999/-	$ 207,100/-

Appendix (4)

Sonia Amer trade mark Logo, it is a baby African elephant with its proboscis up, it means the hope and the green life.

Bag your life

Appendix (5)

The organization chart of Sonia Amer trademark 2009-2011:

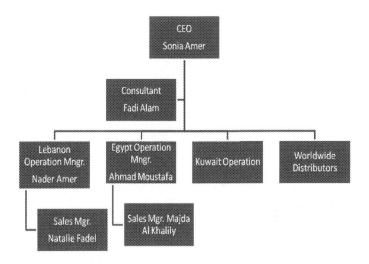

Note: The names mentioned in the organizational chart are not real, except Sonia. The real names of the team are confidential

Appendix (6)

The direct competitors list of prices:

Leather Palace				
Brand	**Size of bag**	**Color**	**Kind of the skin**	**Price**
Gucci	Big bag	Black	Baby caw, crocodile style	$ 750
Cromina	Medium bag	Red	Baby caw, crocodile style	$400
Guy la Roche	Medium	brown		$300
Just Caroll	Big bag	black	Cobra skin	$ 450
Pontatrace	Big bag	Off white	Goat plus cobra	$ 480

The indirect competitors list:

Herms handbags				
	Length	Color	Kind of Skin	Price
1	35 cm	Blue	Ostrich	$1,300.00
2	30 cm	Sea blue	Croc	$4,200.00
3	28 cm	Black	Fur	$459.00
4	32 cm	Red	-	$459.00
Louis Vuitton				
	Model of the bag			Price
1	Monogram	Mirror silver	Speedy bag	$175.00
2	No made	-	Kee pail	$265.00
3	Onatah	Yellow	GM	$194.00
4	Pochette	Yellow	Accessories	$138.00
Gucci				
	Model of the bag			Price
1	Guccissima	85th anniversary bag	Dark brown	$170.00
2	Gucci Moon	Bag medium	pink alligator	$160.00
3	Guccissima Medium	Hobo	Fuchsia	$178.00
4	Web strap	Boston white	Ostrich	$186.00
YSL				
	Model of the bag	Color	Kind of the skin	price
1	Rive gauche	Light brown	Ostrich	$225.00

Resource: West Handbags, The Best Fashion Source For Your Designer Handbags, http://www.handbagshoe.com/designer%20handbags/hermes%20handbags.html (Last accessed in March 22, 2009).

Appendix (7)

The leaflet distributed through the electronic campaign, may 2010:

Resource: Sonia Amer trademark archives, designed by the Gulf Web Company.

Appendix (8)

The decision tree, resource, Sonia Amer trademark's
Business plan 2011-2012.

Decision Tree			
		Excellent Leather	
	Egypt		Reasonable Price
		Poor Finishing	
		Poor Leather	
	Morocco		Expensive
		Good Finishing	
Manufacturing		Fine Leather	
Sonia Amer ™	Lebanon		Expensive
Leather source of Origin		Good Finishing	
Overhead Cost		Fine Leather	
	Syria		Reasonable Price
		Poor Finishing	
		Fine leather	
	Turkey		Expensive
		Good Finishing	

Appendix (9)

NCR REPORT

NCR S.N. (S.N .shall be filled by QA function Only):	
Auditor: ISO Clause No.:	Function/Department: Auditee: Date of audit:
NCR/Observation details:	
Auditee signature:	Date:

Resource, Sonia Amer trademarks' audit conducted, November, 2011.